Zen Conservatism

By

William Hennessy

Also by William Hennessy

The Conservative Manifesto

In memory of

Amie Hennessy

Daddy misses you, sweetie

and dedicated to

my love, Ace

Contents

Acknowledgements

I started this book in November 2008, just after the election. I didn't tell my wife, but she figured out I was up to something. She encouraged me and picked up the slack I left behind without complaint . . . without even mentioning it.

My kids are used to my many flaws, disappearing into projects being one of those. They maintained without me during a year of writing and protests.

My sisters, Mary, Sue, and Mickey, were helping my Dad cope with my Mom throughout the writing of this book. They did my job, and they still do. They sustain our movement and help at every event. No annoying little brother could ask for better sisters than mine.

Dad, hang in there. I love you.

Everyone needs a *consigliere* and Dr. Gina Loudon has, without fanfare or compensation, become that for me in the matters of this book and the Tea Party movement. I know where I'd be without her—pulling out hair and doubting everything. Thanks, Gina.

Dana Loesch was famous when I emailed her on February 21, 2009. I was anything but. She spun up a whirlwind of deadlines and publicity, and next thing I knew we were leading a movement. She has been the energy and the light of the St. Louis Tea Party since day one. Without her, there'd have been no summer of patriotic resistance and 10,000 person rallies. She has opened doors and filled them with great things, and her contribution to the cause of liberty in America will go down in history.

John Loudon reminds me of a brother—the responsible, good looking, talented brother—I never had. I'm amused when, in his company, someone says, "Senator." I mean, it's really cool and privilege to hang out with a retired State Senator and one with an admirable record. Stellar, even. It's even cooler that he's way more John Loudon, friend, fellow Cold War buff. Thanks, John.

Ed Martin Jr. will be a Congressman soon, God willing. He deserves it, and the people of Missouri's 3rd deserve him.

Michelle Moore was another of the first faces to say, "I'll help" on Facebook when the Tea Party began. Thank you.

Darin Morley, the official Tea Party video director, has been a counterweight. He diplomatic explains, "Bill, maybe we should sing hymns *before* we light the torches and charge into the Capitol Building." Without him, I'd probably be under house arrest awaiting my appeal.

Quincy Dave—where would we be without you? You make the Dark Arts seem holy.

Sharp Elbows (Adam Sharp) and Rob "Patch" Adams have made our movement delightful. Not for us, for the millions who watch their fantastic video.

Doug Edelman and Jim Durbin have moved mountains with little recognition, but much deserved. Doug, like Dana, has a knack for opening doors. So does Durbin, but the doors he opens usually say "Carnahan" on the door and hide hideous government corruption. Our Bob Woodward.

Ed Schultz I knew before the Tea Party, but not the way I do now. If at 2 o'clock in the morning I said, "we need a back hoe," Ed would make a phone call and the heavy machinery would appear before the cock crowed three. A tireless working and resourceful agent for the republic, his place in history will be high or low depending on which sides—right or left—writes the book.

Michael Patrick Leahy is the Jedi master of the Tea Party and of Rules for Conservative Radicals. He has made the movement possible and deserves much praise from free people everywhere.

In St. Louis, thousands upon thousands work endlessly to restore the republic. I thought I was alone, but I've learned I was wrong. Thank you. I know too many of your names to begin listing them—I have to keep the page count reasonable to keep the price reasonable. But you, too, are the men and women of the next volume in the American Revolution. This book's for you.

Finally, to God and our Savior, who gave me a family that valued education, teachers who wouldn't let me play when there were lessons to be learned, coaches who taught the value of losing in preparing to win, friend, peers, and bosses who pushed me on and on, thank you all.

Wildwood, MO

December 9, 2009

Introduction

"I know that I am leaving the winning side for the losing side, but it is better to die on the losing side than to live under Communism."

--Whittiker Chambers's Statement before the House Un-American Activities Committee, August 3, 1948

Follow me to the banks of Mississippi River where cobblestones slope into the brown murk that separates St. Louis, Missouri, from East St. Louis, Illinois. Watch your step on the stones as you descend the levy toward the water—it isn't far. You'll have to watch for cars parked haphazardly on the levy.

Now stop, just short of the water, and look across the river to the other side. Rust and concrete with black, arrow-head stains and high, dead smokestacks line the Illinois side.

Turn around. See the Gateway Arch covered in mirrors, glazed with Elmer's glue and water to dull the shine. See the buildings beyond that continue growing as you watch, like a time-lapse of an oak tree in a Discovery Channel documentary. Across the river, you see government. Big government. To the West, you see enterprise. You stand between.

Winston Churchill, while touring Canada as Prime Minister, visited one of the provinces where he attended a dinner in his honor. Beside him sat a Methodist preacher who, like Churchill, was born in the 19th century. Unlike Churchill, the minister had no time for chat. He barely spoke to the Prime Minister before or during dinner. The minister barely moved.

A waitress rounded an oaken corner into the dark, ornate, Victorian dining room. She carried a large tray of sherry in glasses. She went straight to the guest of honor and offered a glass.

"Oh, thank you, lassie," the Prime Minister said. "Your timing couldn't have been better."

Next the waitress lowered the tray before the Methodist preacher. The minister revolted.

"How dare you!" he told the young woman. "How dare you push that poison on a man of the cloth? I would sooner commit *adultery* with you than to violate my being with the Devil's drink."

The young waitress blushed; she settled the tray to leave the room, but Churchill grabbed her arm.

"Lassie," he said, lifting his glass of sherry toward the young woman. "Take mine, too. I am appalled—you didn't tell me I had that choice."

Every day we choose, not between sherry and a hot, young waitress, but between dependence and self-reliance. We choose between slavery to government and slavery to God. We choose between distraction and focus, license and duty, complexity and beauty, death and life, statism and liberty. Please follow deeper into the heart of these contrasting choices.

Many choices you'll make will not seem as stark as St. Louis and East St. Louis. Many decisions seem to pit a greater evil against a lesser one, or a great good against another good. Rarely, though, are choices so subtle, no matter their appearance. Don't be fooled. Don't take any decision lightly. Eve's decision seemed benign, after all: a perfectly healthy looking fruit or obedience to some distant Deity who left her to her own devices. She chose, and her choice made all the difference in the world.

Recall the quote from Whittaker Chambers at the start of this chapter. While his choice to leave communism and fight it did not halt communism's advance, it might have slowed it a bit.

Another communist turned capitalist, James Burnham, gave communism an American edge. When he parted with communism, he took his influence to our side, just as did Whittaker Chambers and John Dos Passos had previously. Later, Michael Savage, David Horowitz, P. J. O'Rourke, and countless others would abandoned their dream of a single, all-powerful world government for libertarianism, or its cousin—a republic.

In moving right, these men made difficult choices, as we learned from Whittaker Chambers in "Witness." Imagine choosing to abandon the ideology and political form you'd advocated for a lifetime. Imagine being a traitor—a true traitor—to a cause you once considered the most important in all humanity. When a statist turns to liberty, his friends turn against him. Some plot his assassination. Others use toadies in the press to spread hideous lies to destroy the traitor's reputation. Organizations opposed to liberty hire proxies who attempt to seduce the traitor, his spouse, and his children. They target the escapee for ridicule, hatred, and death.

You don't have to be Catholic to understand the church's warnings to the pious: that evil will tempt the holiest among us, for the good are doubly troublesome to evil's goals. The devil tempted Christ in the desert, and again in Gethsemane. When a famous preacher falls to temptation, the victory for the Devil is double. Why would he bother with the lukewarm Christians who go to church most Sundays and live decent lives guided, not by faith, but by fear of losing their status?

Likewise, the statist views the ordinary American with contempt, but ignores him. Those common folk who want only to be left alone from politics, collect their Social Security at 65, and retire to a nice condo in Boca

Vista Phase II are already doing their job by the statist. The banal middle class dutifully parrots the evening news about Global Warming and waterboarding at Guantanamo Bay, drones on senselessly about the "healthcare crisis" in America, and takes its offspring to soccer, ballet, play dates, and the psychologist. Most Americans are as much a threat to statism as a garter snake is to an elephant.

The statist targets, instead, the pillars of free markets and the champions of free people. Statists attack entrepreneurs, business people, investors, Christians, conservatives, libertarians, the pious, Joe the Plumber, Sarah Palin, Ronald Reagan, and people who voice their opinions through tea parties.

At the same time, statists exploit and celebrate addicts, terrorists, pornographers, the lazy, welfare queens, murderers, and perverts. In general, statists—or liberals as most of us inaccurately call them—worship wickedness.

Choices. To get a job, or to live off the work of others? To raise a child, or to have it ground up *in utero* with the surgical equivalent of beaters? To live free or die?

You and others will determine whether or not this republic will survive or perish from the earth. The choice is yours . . . .for a little while, anyway.

About every seven years, the Arizona desert gets soaked in the fall and winter. The following spring, something remarkable happens: the desert flower springs to life. Thousands of flower species explode in color. The grayish brown desert looks more like a municipal park in the Midwest.

In the other, normal years, the desert shows a very quiet Spring dance. The seeds are there. The potential for life abounds, but a lack of rain keeps the flowers subdued.

Conservatism is like the desert in this regard. Conservatives are more comfortable sitting back and enjoying life. We're not activist by nature. We're not passive, either, be we don't seek confrontation and turmoil the way statists do. Attempt to steal our freedom, though, and our militant anger blossoms like the dormant desert after a heavy rain.

The past few years have been a deluge of government irresponsibility and expansion. While Washington's been driving blind, the executives and directors of our largest corporations have been driving drunk. Whatever they teach at Harvard's business school clearly destroys the common sense of the students. Goldman Sachs has manipulated the stock market for years, reaping billions—if not trillions—in profits from other people's misery. General Motors, for decades, caved into ridiculous and irresponsible union demands until it collapsed under the weight of its own cowardice. Same for Chrysler. The list of economic, governmental, and fiduciary atrocities could fill a book. But not this one. This one is about the choice before us:

Live Free

Or

Die

Why Zen Conservatism?

The Founders envisioned a zen government.

Seriously. What else would you call a government constrained by a constitution to do only that bare minimum necessary for the good order of the several states? The United States was the occidental world's first minimalist government. The delegates to the convention in Philadelphia, and the champions for ratification in the state legislatures, were zen masters. Or masters of zen government, if you prefer.

As a Christian and a conservative, I have no use for the religious beliefs of Zen Buddhism. Yet Zen offers something that I find lacking in modern American society: elimination of the unnecessary. By "unnecessary," I mean unnecessary material goods, thoughts, commitments, tasks, processes, phobias, conflicts, and aspirations. While it's up to the individual to decide what is or is not necessary in his life, I fear few actively consider the question at all. Instead, we seek simply "more."

This minimalist approach also encourages us to focus on the hard, cold truths about ourselves, our world, and the movement. We can look at two periods of rapid statist ascendancy, to help determine the urgency of our present situation.

In 1964, the first conservative candidate for president, Barry Goldwater of Arizona, was trounced by statist Democrat Lyndon Johnson. Goldwater's was one of the most lopsided defeats in history. The press immediately, and for years thereafter, pronounced conservatism dead.

Two years later, and two days after Ronald Reagan became the governor of California, Goldwater was a guest on William F. Buckley's *Firing Line* on CBS. Listening, now, to Goldwater's thoughts of 40 years ago warms the conservative heart. Despite statist domination of both houses of Congress, the Supreme Court, and the White House, conservatives were able to thwart some statist initiatives, for sure. More importantly, the conservatives of the 1960s laid the foundation and built the organizations for Ronald Reagan's 1980 triumph and for Newt Gingrich's rescue of Congress in 1994. The decade and a half between Reagan's victory in California and his victory across the nation was something like Israel's time in the desert. Without a period of penance, reflection, and prayer, conservatives would not have been ready to govern.

In 1976, Ronald Reagan narrowly lost the Republican nomination to liberal Republican Gerald

Ford. Ford used the GOP's old boys' network to secure the party's nod, while Reagan relied on popular support among conservative academics and blue collar voters, many of whom were Democrats willing to cross party lines to vote for the popular California governor. Reagan used California, and it's huge economy, as a laboratory for conservative economics. As governor, he managed to guarantee a college education to every Californian who could get accepted while balancing the budget and cutting taxes. Conservatism simply worked.

After Reagan's narrow defeat at the hands of incumbent President Gerald Ford in '76, pundits, again, called conservatism dead. But reports of its death were greatly exaggerated. Four years later, Reagan would defeat Ivy Leaguer George Bush for the Republican nomination, toss the statist anti-Semite, Jimmy Carter, out of office, and go on to become one of the most popular presidents in history. Reagan launched the longest, sustained economic rally America has ever seen. Once again, conservatism worked.

The founding principles of life, liberty, pursuit of happiness, and private property are as alive today as they were in 1966 and 1976. That's both good news and bad: those principles were far less popular in '66 and '76 than they were in 1982 or 2002. We've taken a big step backwards, for sure, but we haven't fallen off a cliff. Yet.

And we have the shoulders of giants to stand upon and see the Promised Land.

So let's stop whining, and go out there and win one for the Gipper.

Warm-ups

Before we dig into the meat of the book, you need to get ready with a quick warm-up. This won't hurt a bit, and it won't embarrass you publicly, I promise.

With all the pressures of modern life, we need to relax. Did you know that it is impossible to learn something new when your mind is under severe stress or fear? Did you know that worry (anxiety) and fear will cause you to freeze rather than fight or flee if you don't know what to do?

This book will try to give you some tactics, but more importantly it will try to calm the political storms in your mind for a bit. Sure, it will also stir them up. But you'll have tools to manage the political stress you face both while reading this text and afterwards. Follow this chapter, and you'll be set.

For further lessons in relaxation in minimalism, see the books and web sites at the end of the chapter.

First, I want you to read this book somewhere beautiful if you can. Somewhere with nature in front of you. Somewhere quiet and relaxing. You don't have to, of course; you could read it in the unhygienic stall of a men's room in a run-down gas station 85 miles west of Helena, Montana. But because this book is intended to let conservatism's simple beauty spread its wings and take flight, I'd like you to read most of the book surrounded by beauty.

Second, I ask that you read the book early in the morning, before exposing yourself to news, blogs, and life's other nabobs of negativity. That's because the news tends to make us angry and cynical. This book is about happiness and magic. Freeing yourself from the negativity of news for a few hours a day while you think about the concepts and prescriptions I present will make your life a little better--even if nothing else comes of it.

Third, take a walk before you read. I ask this because a walk relieves stress and opens the mind to higher things, to the magic that surrounds us everywhere, to the sounds and smells and sights that we tend to rush past without a second thought. Conservatism is, in its soul, the magic of what is. But if we don't take a moment to take in what is, we condemn ourselves to a life of reaching for what we don't have. And that's a prescription for disappointment and bad debt.

Moving Up

The highest compliment a human being can receive is the tacit acknowledgement that he can be trusted to live his own life without the arbitrary rule of other men. Classical liberalism, libertarianism, and conservatism believe men are best ruled by God and their consciences. The purpose of government is not to rule, but to protect and to serve according to the consent of the governed.

These three ideologies, if 'ideology' be the appropriate noun, represent political manifestations of man's highest compliment. These three, which we'll call 'conservatism' for convenience, believe that you are better than your government thinks you are. We conservatives believe in you—the statists believe in government.

When we remove the artificial shackles of government rule from men born free by God's will, we elevate man, not to divinity, but to the thing prescribed by the Divine. We say to our fellows, "we trust you." No one of any other political stripe would be so bold—perhaps because they trust not themselves.

Are you ready? Have you warmed up? Is your mind open to the possibility of making the world better than it's ever been?

Then turn the page and open up to Zen Conservatism.

Further reading:

Blog: Zen Habits blog: www.zenhabits.net

Books: The Power of Less by Leo Babauta

            The 4-Hour Work Week by Timothy
Ferriss

Restoring the Republic

I turned 45 years old in a few months back. With my wife asleep on the couch and the kids scattered around home or town doing their own things, I wandered out onto the deck to take a quick inventory of my life.

It's easy, as one gets older, to feel sorry for himself. Well, maybe it's not feeling sorry for oneself as much as regretting some of the decisions we've made. That lasted about five seconds.

I looked up through a couple of holes in the clouds that covered St. Louis that evening, and I saw the brightest damn stars set against blue-black midnight sky. That self-pity and self-recrimination faded in a second. Instead of missed opportunities and bad decisions, in that star I saw eternal hope; in the heavens behind it, boundless opportunity.

The greatest discoveries and finest inventions of my lifetime are not behind me—they're somewhere before me. The greatest moments in American history didn't happen in a history book I read in grade school, but are gestating inside the minds and hearts of our sons and daughters. That star is our future, and the field on which it shines a stage.

Many of wondrous things have happened in my life. We "broke the surly bonds of earth" to explore space, the moon, and Mars. We put computers in every home and connected them together with a global internetwork. We have cell phones that put us in communication with anyone, anywhere, anytime. And that's just a few technological achievements.

In my lifetime, we've wiped out diseases and gained the upper hand on many others. We've knocked back evil communism to a containable few square miles here and there. We've deposed despots, as Americans have for centuries, and we've managed to do it without become despots ourselves.

Still, we've only scratched the surface of our potential.

For most of my life, these accomplishments and the ones that came before them and made them possible, relied on only about 30 percent of the American population. Women and blacks comprised 61percent of the US population most of life, yet for most of our history we ignored their potential contributions. Add in Hispanics and immigrants from other countries, and the population allowed to contribute to our greatness was even smaller.

Some look at the fact of our past stupidity and say it proves us weak. I look at our accomplishments despite such shortcomings and say it proves us great. In this century, we can accomplish 60 percent more than we did in the last without working any harder. If we can put a man on the moon and cure polio with only white men, imagine what we can do with the whole population.

But we might not accomplish much more.

There are some in our society who think America is a drain on the world, an insult to God and nature, a blight on world history. These people look into the midnight sky and see the stars as weapons aimed on our heads for our misdeeds. Where I see hope, they see guilt. Where I see opportunity, they see curses. Where I see joy, they see avarice.

These people elected Barack Obama.

The hope Obama speaks of isn't hope at all. It's bondage. It's bondage to the failed ideologies that we put down in the Cold War. It's the failed and feeble idea that most people are incapable of making good decisions and doing the right thing. It's a corollary to the belief that the few with intelligence and good judgment are corrupt and use their smarts to take advantage of the rest.

I utterly refute this notion.

If the world is divided into feeble-minded saints and intelligent crooks, then who among us is fit to protect the one from the other? If cognitive agility must manifest itself as cheating and stealing, then the do-gooders are either too stupid to achieve their noble ends or phonies feigning virtue to fool the masses.

In other words, if Barack Obama is right, then Barack Obama must be wrong or stupid.

I've had this problem with statists since I was about 10 years old. They always want to protect us from some possible danger, and they always want us to cede a bit of our freedom to them. They want us to believe that only they can protect us from the nameless forces that wish us harm. And if we'll give them our power, they'll use it for good.

So we gave them the New Deal and the Great Society and Medicare, Medicaid, Aid to Families with Dependent Children, the minimum wage, food stamps, and countless other programs, yet they tell us that poverty and inequity are worse now than ever before.

How could that be?

We gave them Détente and surrendered South Vietnam, but the Soviet Union just marched on to Afghanistan, Nicaragua, and El Salvador. How could that be? The statists promised that if we stopped shooting the commies, they'd retreat.

The statists were wrong.

But we had a president who said, "enough!" He stood at the Brandenburg Gate and demanded that it be opened. And it was. He stood before Congress and demanded it give back to the people some of the powers that Congress and the Courts had usurped. And Congress obeyed. He stood before the American people and said, "I believe in you," and his faith was vindicated a thousand times over in the next 15 years.

We seem to have lost some of the magic that president gave us. We seem, once again, to be questioning the virtue and wonder of this shining city on a hill. Many of us seem very willing–almost eager–to surrender ourselves to some despot who promises to use OUR power, OUR rights, OUR strengths on our behalf.

Don't be that lazy or cowardly. Only a coward would cede his God-given rights to some scrawny wimp egghead to use, supposedly, on our behalf. We are Americans. We take care of ourselves and of the world around us. We don't need government to protect us from the unnamed, unseen enemies who might harm us. We need government only to protect us from the enemies WITH names and faces. We'll take care of the rest ourselves.

To do that, though, we must choose actions different from those we've chosen since 1984 and 1994. We must choose and move. And we must bring along multitudes of people who are now politically asleep.

Let's Move Up

MoveOn.org formed in 1998. Its name shouted at conservatives who were clamoring for Bill Clinton's impeachment. "Move on," it said, "to important matters."

Unfortunately for everyone who yearns to breathe the air of freedom, MoveOn.org ignored its own message. Clinton was retained in office, his prosecutors moved on, but the statists at MoveOn only got angrier, more hateful, further bent on ripping down the United States and rebuilding it in their own funhouse mirror-image and likeness.

MoveOn, if we can believe the media, is changing its name. Perhaps to "MoveOut." It seems the left wants this country to itself. It seeks freedom from dissent, from the truth, and from consequences.

If we on the right do not want to move out of our country--a country we love more than the left does--then we have important work to do. Our mantra might be "MoveUp," as in "Up From Liberalism."

This book presents a new way to look upon the task before us. Striving for simplicity, it asks pro republic patriots to focus on a few important tasks:

1) Choose 5 important principles to advance

2) Choose 2 important causes to support financially

3) Choose 1 mantra to unify our forces, identify our brand, and remind us of our mission

The road back to political relevancy requires that we reduce, not expand. We must eliminate distractions and focus on now. The future arrives one day at a time, and our enemies hold high offices. A big tent that gives quarter to those who would dilute our message and dissipate our energies on meaningless things works against us. It's just a knock of what the Democrats, socialists, and communists have pushed for decades. To restore our republic, we must consolidate our strengths, expand our numbers, focus our energies, and exploit the enemy's myriad weaknesses.

This Book

Zen Conservatism encourages conservatives to recognize our own drift toward licentiousness and distraction, and our fascination with complexity. This book asks people to reduce the obligations they have accepted. By de-cluttering our minds and our physical environments, reacquainting ourselves with conservatism's basics, and taking definite, daily actions that advance our fundamental principles, we can recapture the march begun by Barry Goldwater and Ronald Reagan in 1964.

If you don't think we need better focus, let's ask three simple questions:

Where's the Fun? Have you noticed that conservative blogs are less informative and less entertaining than they were four, six, or eight years ago? I'm including my own here. One reason is that we don't focus well. We scan everything--every topic, every discipline, and every story. We write pithy, angry responses. We pick things apart and look for malice in even the most innocuous stories and statements. We pay attention to too many distractions, and distractions disrupt careful thought.

What's Our Focus? Jack Kemp campaigned for empowerment through low taxes and limited government. Ronald Reagan advanced smaller government, lower taxes, and a strong foreign policy. What do we promote? Toward what noble end do we march? Without a focus, we're doomed to produce nothing but gripes and country music.

What Do We Stand For? Have you noticed that supposedly conservative leaders don't state long-known truths very often? John McCain ran an entire campaign without ever saying, "Governments don't create wealth--they steal it." How can that be? Is it because he was too busy being all things to all people? Could anyone confidently describe McCain's campaign as "focused?" Distractions disrupt focus.

We stand for the Republic—the tight association of 50 sovereign states who, in 1787 and several times thereafter, delegated certain powers to the United States, an artificial government crafted by the people of the several states.

We stand for liberty—freedom from the arbitrary rule of other men. Liberty is the gift God gave Adam and Eve. Since that heavenly grant, political serpents have stolen man's liberty, imposed arbitrary despotism, and denied man his God-given right to self-governance.

We stand for property—private property, earned through honest labor, disposed according to the owner's wishes, and defended by owners and governments against encroachment and confiscation. Taxation and regulation threaten this standard of American freedom.

If you stand with us, then your labor and toil will leave America free and strong. If you do not choose, a side will be chosen for you.

Focus and the Tea Party Movement

On February 22, 2009, I was putting the finishing touches on this book. Progress slowed because I'd taken on a project at my day job which required 60 to 70 hours of work a week. I had suspended my early rising. I stopped running in the morning and lifting weights in the evening. My family became blurs that passed through my peripheral vision as I worked late into the night and weekends.

On that Sunday, though, I decided that I'd stop work at noon to catch up on my family and the world. I read Michelle Malkin's blog about spontaneous Tea Parties in Chicago and a half dozen other cities. The protests were in response to Rick Santelli's rant against yet another proposed bailout from the White House. My son had sent to me the link to his rant on YouTube.com form the previous Friday. I'd dismissed the whole thing. Too much work to do.

I decided that St. Louis needed a Tea Party, and, through my blog, proposed holding one on March 14 before the annual downtown St. Patrick's Day Parade. I emailed a famous local blogger (Jim Hoft of Gateway Pundit) and a conservative radio talk show hostess,

Dana Loesch, to see if they'd be interested in organizing the event.

Eight hours later, Dana introduced me as the leader of the St. Louis Tea Party to be held at the Gateway Arch the following Friday, February 27.

Since then, my life is changed.

The Tea Party movement is swelling. On Fox News Special Edition, Bret Bair reported on the MSM's reluctance to cover the tea parties, citing an Investor's Business Daily story: "The real reason the major media aren't interested in these protests is that they don't agree with them."

If the major media are against us, we're doing something right.

The statists in both parties who run our government seek to maximize their power and minimize ours. They hope to make the United States nothing more than a sheepish, cowed, socialist land of obsequious myrmidons. No one in Washington will stand up to them.

But we will. We know that man is endowed with rights as natural as breathing. We don't need college classes on Life, Liberty, and the Pursuit of Happiness, anymore than we need classes on waking up. Freedom is our natural state.

Some statists claim that progress requires us to surrender freedom, individualism, and the time of our lives to an all-powerful government. Sorry, but that's not progress; that's regress. If man's natural state is freedom, bondage is not a step forward.

So never stop recruiting. We need the participation of every person who yearns freedom and human dignity, regardless of party affiliation or prior understanding of his or her ideology. We need all the women, blacks, Hispanics, Asians, Objectivists, Libertarians, gays, and even Cub fans. In this battle, conservatism isn't political—it's moral.

In his introduction to "God and Man at Yale," William F. Buckley wrote that the battle between individualism and collectivism is the same battle as God vs. Satan, fought on a different plane. Your participation in the Tea Party movement is a moral choice. You and your family should be proud of what you're doing.

For those of you who haven't joined, please consider this question: when the gangs of thugs come after your home, when the government taxes 90 percent of your income, when inflation hits 20 percent a year, will you still believe that soccer games and "American Idol" were more important than restoring our republic?

Here's an example of the kind of emails I've been getting since that February Tea Party:

> I hope you don't mind me bugging you

> about this but I've been trying to find a
> group to get involved in that understands
> that some people have principles and they
> don't believe government is the answer to
> the mess we are in. I would really like any
> information you have on getting connected
> with like minded people.

Add to that the dozens of people who approached me on the Arch grounds in St. Louis last February and said, "I've been afraid to speak up. I was afraid people would ridicule me or my job would be threatened. When I saw this, I realized I can finally speak my mind."

Statists in America have waged a 30-year war on free speech in which the only acceptable speech is that which perpetuates leftist lies, slanders conservatism, denigrates the United States, accuses our Armed Forces, ridicules Judeo-Christian values, or vilifies business owners who put food on tables and roofs over our heads.

ENOUGH!

I don't care what statists think about my views anymore. I won't go out of my way to pick a fight, of course, but I'm not going to let lies go unchallenged. I am no longer willing to let my tax dollars to to ACORN and other statist groups to be used against me. I am no longer willing to keep my mouth shut when the Chris

Matthews and Campbell Brown lie about America in order to advance socialism. I am done being a patsy for Communist atheists who want to turn America into Sudan. I am done being scared.

I'm sick of living in a country where children are taught to steal from the "rich." I'm fed up with whiny welfare ladies and lords demanding more confiscation of my income in order to benefit bums. If ACORN's members were to put half the energy into productive labor that they put into demanding that others pay their ways through life, they'd be richer than Bill Gates.

Health insurance is not a right. A right is something you'd have if you were alone an island. There you could say anything you want, build the hut of your dreams, kill the beasts that roam the land and the fish that swim in the sea and lagoon. You could make a rule for yourself that you will rise with the sun each morning, write 10 filthy words in the sand on the beach, and drink 18.5 fluid ounces of the ale you've learned to brew using native grasses and grains. All the things you lacked comprise that enormous body of that which IS NOT A RIGHT!

Our government was instituted BY US to ensure that we remained as free as if we were the ONLY PERSON ON THE ISLAND. On the island, you wouldn't have free health care except for that which you practiced yourself. You wouldn't have a free home except the one you built yourself. You wouldn't have a free car unless you managed to build one yourself. You wouldn't have a court to sanction a gull for his mocking reproaches that offend your self-esteem.

Because our founders understood that governments are more prone to encroaching on your freedman than are your neighbors, they gave us a Constitution that sets out a very small number of specific tasks which government may perform, forbidding the government from doing anything else. Read the 10th Amendment then Article 1. You'll start to get it.

And no group has a moral right to steal things from one of its members, even after a fair and democratic vote. Imagine if your co-workers took a vote at lunch and decided that you'll pay the entire bill no matter what anyone ate. Their justification, "You had a vote, Phil. It just didn't go your way. Buck up and pay for our lunches."

But Congress does just that. It votes to force some people to pay for other people's lunches! You cannot justify it. You can't. Smarter people than you have tried and they've failed utterly.

So knock off the entitlement crap and the whining about the rich. In most cases, the rich got that way because they spent less than they earned. Tough formula, huh? If you make $100, spend $80. Next time do the same. And again and again and again. Pretty soon you'll have a POSITIVE NET WORTH. With America's savings rate and marginal propensity to consume over the past 20 years, you only need about $100 to be considered rich!

Before you think I'm being holier than thou, think again. I guarantee you that I've been more reckless with money than you. I have chased pipe dreams and lived way beyond my means. I've lost a home and cars and family chasing Madison Avenue's American Dream when I should have been chasing James Madison's. If there's an authority on irresponsible living, it's me.

If you find yourself in a dire financial problem, do what has always worked: spend less, live simply, sell things you don't need, augment your income with odd jobs, pay down your debt, cut up your credit cards, put off new purchases. If you think you can't do those things, go to the authority: Dave Ramsey (www.daveramsey.com). Dave has books and online programs that work wonders at uncovering what you already know about money: you can't borrow your way to prosperity anymore than the government can.

The next time you hear someone say, "The government should do this; why doesn't the government take care of that?" speak UP. Respond! Say, "You ARE the friggin' government, honey, why the hell don't YOU do something about it? If it's so damned important, then why wait for some mindless bureaucrat to fix it? Get off your miraculously spreading rump and take care of it yourself."

And for those in the national media and the idiots who parrot everything they say: I didn't have time to tell my sisters, cousins, nephews, or even my WIFE about this Tea Party thing, it happened so fast. I was minding my own damned business that Sunday–something the statists know NOTHING about–when I decided to put out feelers about having a protest against government spending. Dana Loesch, at the time a Sundy evening radio talk host and a blog author on Mamalogues.com and DanaRadio.com, offered to team up with me. So many angry and frightened people responded to my blog post and Dana's radio announcement by saying, "I'm in" that we had no choice but to take my advice and DO SOMETHING ABOUT IT OURSELVES!!!!. We conservatives don't have government bureaus we can petition to stop government stupidity. We have to take matters into our own hands.

And after a week of working 50 hours at my day job while organizing a protest on 12 hours sleep in 5 nights (same conditions for Dana, by the way) the statists accused us of a) being billionaires and b) planning this thing for 2 years! Hell, we got 1,500 people marching in 4 days! With 2 years and a billion dollars, we'd have taken over Congress!

And we will take over the Congress in 2010, so help us God!

Now, visit www.nationwideteapartycoalition.com to find out how you can get involved.

Since that cold day in February when over 1,000 patriots gathered on the steps of the Arch in St. Louis and over 40,000 Americans protested government growth, spending, taxing, and borrowing in more than 40 cities, the movement has grown rapidly.

On April 15, 2009, more than one millions protested nationwide at the Tax Day Tea Party. Fox News covered the event live from San Antonio, Atlanta, New York, and other cities. Within weeks, the movement was gnawing on Barack Obama's mind when he told a crowd at Fox High School in Arnold, Missouri, "Those of you who are watching certain news channels on which I am not very popular and you see folks waving tea bags around."

The Tea Party movement exemplifies focus. Participating in the national movement also reveals just how vigilant we must be in keeping focused on our goals.

Tea Party organizers (servant-leaders) receive thousands of emails every week, many wanting the movement to push pro-life, pro-military, anti-immigration, and a host of other issues. If we do, the movement will fail.

The focus of the Tea Party movement is grass roots activism to disrupt government borrowing (repeal the pork) and to win a conservative majority in both houses of Congress in 2010 (retire the borrowers). That's enough.

Where We Stand

The Tyranny of "More"

Our pursuit of "more" has put us in a difficult and unsustainable position. (As much as I detest the word "unsustainable," it precisely describes the state of our culture.) Want and desire have replaced reason. People saw more, then pursued more, then expected more, and, finally, demanded more. One need only look at the financial meltdown of 2008 to see the results of this rush to more:

Home values plunged;

Stock market values fell by half;

Major investment banks disappeared overnight;

Unemployment grew faster than economists could revise their predictions;

The US auto industry collapsed;

Commercial banks, large and small, melded faster than drops of mercury.

Economists and others pondered the reasons for these results, looking primarily at the financial risk and economic causes. Conservatives correctly blamed Congress for Freddie Mac and Fannie Mae--

governmental bureaucracies that ran amok with financial risk. Freddie and Fannie's irresponsible policies led banks to irresponsible behavior. Investment banks hid risk inside investment grade securities, institutions bought the securities, the risks were realized, and -- poof-- trillions of dollars of value vanished like fog in a river valley burned off by the hot morning sun.

What few analysts studied about the meltdown was behavior driven by attitudes. When we look here we find the true cause of the meltdown: rampant want of more. We cannot blame Congress or Morgan Stanley or even Bernie Madoff. These institutions and individuals fed us what we wanted. We demanded cheap money with which to buy more stuff.

With borrowed money, we bought bigger houses in better neighborhoods with higher property taxes and pretentious neighbors. I have a 42-inch LCD 1080p HDTV, four computers, and a $2,000 stove. We have gigantic, 8-passenger SUVs for our families of three, and five-hundred-dollar cell phones that duplicate our computer's functions.

We pay two hundred dollars for baseball tickets where multi-millionaires play a game that kids used to play for free--before GameBoys stole their time, attention, and childhood as they help Luigi navigate killer mushrooms.

We borrowed our way into isolation, ignorance, and poverty. Now we're surrounded by things we do not need and lack the things we really crave—freedom, liberty, and opportunity. So worried are we about our material gadgets that many continue to trade more of our liberties to the government in Washington in exchange for a false sense of security. We seem willing to trust government to live our lives and to supply our happiness.

Corporate CEOs who claim to love free markets fly to Washington to beg the government to confiscate from our children's tomorrow in order to pay performance bonuses today. Sanator John McCain calls these raids "the generational theft act." Stealing is immoral whether it's done by government or by a crack head.

Peggy Noonan noticed our deadly pursuit of more in a 1998 essay, "There is No Time; There Will Be Time." The essay became famous after 9/11 because Noonan seemed to predict such an event, and its aftermath.

About life in America in the late 1990s—which has grown only worse since—Noonan wrote:

> All our splendor, our comfort, takes time to pay for. And affluence wants to increase; it carries within it an unspoken command: More!

Affluence is like nature, which always moves toward new life. Nature does its job; affluence enlists us to do it. We hear the command for "More!" with immigrant ears that also hear "Do better!" or old American ears that hear, "Sutter is rich, there's gold in them hills, onward to California!" We carry California within us; that is what it is to be human, and American.

Later, ominously, she tells us what's to come:

Something's up. And deep down, where the body meets the soul, we are fearful. We fear, down so deep it hasn't even risen to the point of articulation that with all our comforts and amusements, with all our toys and bells and whistles . . . we wonder if what we really have is . . . a first-class stateroom on the Titanic. Everything's wonderful, but a world is ending and we sense it.

In 2001, everyone who read this thought the "big, terrible thing" was 9/11. But it wasn't. The terrorist attack that killed 3,000 Americans and launched two wars on a brilliant blue day in September is now a blip on our national memory. Like when Seattle Slew won the Triple Crown or when some little kid was rescued from a well.

Since 9/11, we've gone back to the break-neck rat race that Noonan railed against in her essay.

I work between 50 and 80 hours a week. My kids don't participate in many afterschool activities, because I couldn't shuttle them around. But I constantly feel like things are coming apart. I seek distractions like everyone else.

Perhaps what Noonan foresaw was not 9/11, but Barack Obama and a statist Congress. Together, they can give us a lot of time.

Or maybe she foresaw something even more horrible: nuclear Iran, with its overt desire to give America an Electromagnetic Pulse (EMP) attack that would fry out everything electrical in North America. There would be no radio, television, computer, cell phone, printer, automobile (newer than about 1960 model year), water, electricity, gasoline pumps, pacemakers, EKGs, EEGs, MRIs, or airplanes.

Could Peggy have spotted some biomedical terror unleashed by a careless worker at the CDC or the Defense Department's germ warfare labs? Possibly. Although she could also have seen nano technology unleash some silicon nightmare artificial virus that crawls through our pores and eats our brains—and there's nothing anyone can do to stop it.

The reason Zen Conservatism begs you to slow down, throw out, and focus is because something big and ugly still seems poised to strike out, and the distracted will be the first to go. Eliminate the unnecessary now, while it still matters.

Let's be very clear: by "things they do not need," I do not pretend to make myself the final arbiter of necessity or happiness. I do not mean that some objective evaluation can determine what a person needs or doesn't need. I do mean that we collected crap we ourselves didn't really need or even want. I'll use myself as a perfect example:

When I began simplifying my life in November 2008, I put off organizing my clothes closet precisely to avoid embarrassment and self-loathing. I have so many clothes that I cannot stand straight to pull shirts from their hangers--the pile of clothes on the floor prevents it. I have to get on my toes at the closet's edge and lean into the racks, bracing my left hand on a vertical tube while pulling the desired shirt with my right.

I hate to throw away the clothes I don't wear often because most of them I've never worn. They're brand new! Many still have store tags. I bought stuff I'll never wear!

This pattern repeats itself throughout my house: the garage, every closet, the family room, living room, kitchen, bathrooms, basement, storage areas, backyard, refrigerator, cabinets, desks, under beds, in the attic. Everywhere I look I see crap I bought and never or rarely used. Coffee pots that were replaced for no good reason are boxed up and stored only because I feel too guilty to pitch them.

The prescription is simple, and there's a 98 percent chance you know what you have to do: throw it away. Get Leo Babauta's book, Zen to Done, and get it done. Take the full year, as Leo describes. Develop one powerful habit at a time. Get your stuff into one sock, then empty that sock at least once a week, then set your alarm clock for 4:30 a.m. -- wait, that comes later.

The Zen ideal of "only what's necessary" begins with the physical. Remove the junk, the distractions, the trash, the out-of-place nik-nak the thing that should have been pitched ages ago. Remove them now.

Take the Crap-in-View Challenge

If you haven't put the book down already, you will shortly.

I want you to get up from wherever you are, put down this book, and pivot 360° slowly. Begin this scan of your immediate environment up at the ceiling, then work your way to the floor. It might require three or four revolutions.

For every object you see, ask yourself, "would my life be richer or poorer without it?"

If you answered "poorer" to more than half of the objects, you've either simplified your life already, or you would benefit from one more question: when will I use that thing again?

If you haven't already simplified, scan the room again, asking that second question of each object. Chances are, you have no idea if or when you'll use 90 percent of the things in your field of vision.

So do you really need them? Would your life really be poorer without them? Without the clutter, and the additional things to dust? Without that additional nik-nak or furniture piece or whatever it is?

Everything in your immediate environment contributes to your mental inventory list--a list your mind maintains, adjusts, and updates constantly.

That's distraction.

The Wealth of White Space

White space has a value few consider. Designers understand it, though. White space allows the mind to focus on the necessary. On the wall to my right hangs a single Madonna and Child painting--a favorite since childhood--surrounded by a field of white. If I were to put just one more thing on that wall I'd lose some of the beauty of the Blessed Mother and Christ: Our Lady of Perpetual Help.

Coco Chanel understood this concept perfectly: "When accessorizing, always take off the last thing you put on."

There's an old saying that one's desk (or office) is a reflection of what's in his head. The saying is truer than anyone knows. The accumulation of physical crap in my life reflects the accumulation of mental and metaphysical crap in my head.

The Unnecessary Junk in Your Head

Clearing the physical garbage from your environment is step one. It's not an end in itself, but an enabling point for the real work--the work required to restore conservatism to viability. The real solution involves eliminating garbage from our minds, from our magazines, from our blogs, and from our conversations.

Anyone who's read my blog realizes that I am guilty of all the sins this book attempts to eliminate: greed, avarice, accumulation, anger, hatred, shouting, discontent, meanness, laziness . . . the list would go on forever. The point is, I'm not saying that I am better than you. I am not. I am saying that what I have allowed myself to become, conservatism has become. The movement is fat and distracted.

I am also sick of it all. I'm tired of being angry and bitter and cynical. And let's be perfectly honest: I'm damn tired of losing elections and liberty. I'm sick of my statist friends joking about budget growth with Republicans in the White House and Congress. I'm tired of my favorite conservative writers sounding shrill and desperate.

Our shrillness comes from the pressure of holding too much crap in our heads, not hatred in our hearts. Try this experiment:

For the next seven days beginning when you finish this paragraph, eschew news and politics for a week. No blogs, no RSS feeds of blogs, no Drudge Report, no newspaper, no Evening News with Katie Couric, no Fox News, no Google news gadget on your iGoogle page. Nothing. No news on the radio or on iPod. No calls to "Dial-a-News-Story" or lunchtime chats about Obama's 100 days. No "Zen Conservatism." *Ready . . . Go!*

One Week Without News

If you took the challenge, then you probably picked up my little book with some trepidation. Having gone on a news diet after reading "The 4-Hour Work Week," I have an idea how your week went:

Day One: You cheated within a half hour of waking up. You turned on your shower radio to hear, "President Obama cured leprosy . . . ." Then you remembered your challenge and turned it off. Your car radio was tuned to the local conservative talk station--the one that carries Rush Limbaugh or Sean Hannity--and you listened for 2 minutes before remembering your diet. At work you opened your browser and typed "W-W-W dot D-R-U" and Chrome filled in the rest and took you to Drudge where you read (in 42-point red letters) "Ya Know Caroline Kennedy!" By 3:00, you'd pretty much figured out that you're really damned addicted to news and politics. But you're getting better.

Day Two: Your shower radio is set to classic rock, so you shower with little or no news. In your car Motley Crue sings to you "You and me / We're gonna escape tonight / On the run / Under the moonlight / Don't think about nothin' / Don't think about nothin'" And you think, "Oh my God, I need some news." All day long, your fingers itched on your keyboard. You thought about visiting Michelle Malkin, Hot Air, Gateway Pundit. But you resisted the temptation.

Day Three: At 10:30 a.m. you realized that you hadn't thought about the news until you got an email from Jay Sekolaw at American Center for Law and Justice telling you about the Fairness Doctrine. You're proud of yourself, but this email seems really urgent. *Maybe I better read it,* you think. But what could you possibly do about it--whatever it is? Exaclty. Nothing.

Day Four: You're getting ready for bed before the news crosses your mind. You're in such a good mood you refuse to spoil it.

Day Five: No news is good news. You *finally* understand what that stupid cliche means.

Day Six: The monkey you got off your back two days ago returns with a vengeance. It's screaming "news junkie" in your ear. You've been awake ten minutes and you can't take it. You NEED TO KNOW! In the shower, the water sounds like fake ticker-tape machines from the 1960s opening of "Meet the Press." You hear Marvin

Kalb talking about Spiro Agnew's attack on the press. "What year is it?" you blurt to no one. "What's that, dear?" your wife answers from the bedroom. But the craving passes. You maintain and head out the door to do your work.

Day Seven: No cravings. No coughing fits all day. You can breathe easier. You thing: *Did I quit smoking or just give up news?* In the evening, you sit down in a quiet place and review the week. You feel better, stronger than you did just seven days ago. Except for that bout of depression and anger in the shower yesterday, you've had one of the happiest weeks of your life. You feel strong and courageous because you can go a week without news, politics, and blogs. You feel like a child again. Thoughts tend toward happy things and family and pets instead of budget deficits and unemployment numbers. Unless it's unseasonably hot or cold, the concept of global warming means little. You've made it.

Today you saw this book sitting on the table next to your favorite reading chair. You want to pick it up, but you don't want to go back to the old you. Picking up the book, you observe its glossy, smooth cover and consider its font. After a few moments of reflection on the week without politics, you open to page {page #} and begin to read about the week you just had. You think, *this Hennessy's an idiot; it wasn't anything like that.*

Tim Ferriss's book, "The 4-Hour Work Week," might tempt you to give up news altogether, or reduce news consumption to a few headlines a week. I won't tell you not to try. If you're reading this book and made it this far, you're probably a political animal. In that case, you should come away from this exercise knowing that you don't need all the information you've been taking in.

Even if you're a blogger, you probably consume far more information than you need to produce one or two quality blog posts a day. If you're not a political blogger or writer or commentator, then you don't need much. Pick two or three good blogs (www.hennessysview.com is one of my favorites) and ignore the rest. Don't click every hyperlink in every story or every "My Favorites" in the blog roll. Get what you need and move on.

If terrorists fly planes into a building in New York, you'll know soon enough. If President Obama resigns in scandal, you'll know soon enough. The truly important issues of the day are not issue of the day; they're undeniable truths of life in defense of which we will battle the forces of collectivism and atheism just as we battled yesterday and in 1776.

Learn from the mood improvement you experienced in your week *sans* politics. Think about how clean your mind felt on Day Seven. What were your thoughts in those final two days? Were they clearer and more articulate? Did you find answers instead of problems? Did you see the good in people and events instead of only threats and concerns? Did you find it easier to focus on the essentials?

Zen Conservatism is essentials: life, liberty, pursuit of happiness and good government. That's all there is for conservatism. All issues can be boiled down to a single question: "Will it liberate?" All problems can be solved by one person: you.

Now take a deep breath and proceed. You're going to learn the three true threats to America, Western Civilization, and clear thinking. They are License, Distraction, and Complexity.

License

License (or "Licentiousness") is most easily described as the abandonment of shame, the derogation of consequence in a departure from norms and mores. It manifests itself in abortion on demand, federal bailouts of entire business sectors, no-fault divorce, and a government-paid cure for self-inflicted disease. It demands freedom to do whatever without any possibility of negative returns, particularly pangs of conscience. It demands, not freedom, but permissiveness. It weakens and constrains men; it does not liberate.

The best antonym for license is "reason," oddly enough.

License is the enemy of liberty.

License is a thief in the night who steals self worth. License is the crusty needle with worn graduations rubbed off by overuse and plunged greedily into the junkie's arm in the human cesspool of an East St. Louis abandoned red-brick three-story building at 3:27 on Tuesday morning in hot August, just the way the cops found his body four days later.

License is the "medical waste" bucket of dead baby body parts stinking up a Granite City back-alley after the abortionist has done his job of keeping humanity a somewhat exclusive club in the absurdly named Hope Clinic for Women.

License is the young black man speeding in a stolen Escalade when he's killed in hail of police gunfire at midnight in Normandy just six years after his soon-to-be-grieving mother (a good, church-going woman) was so proud to show off the photograph of his infectious smile in his football uniform when he made the freshmen team after he worked eight hours a day to bring his grades up.

License is the bank statement of the Harvard MBA who won a hundred million dollars for bankrupting his company and putting four-thousand people out of work because the MBA talked the workers into investing their whole 401(k) in the company he destroyed.

License is easy to feel but difficult to see. Abortion is a license to kill. Promiscuity, in general, is license: a license causes social problems.

The conservative must recognize license if only to distinguish it from reason. God gives us the freedom to do any good we wish. He does not give us the freedom to do wrong, but He does give us the ability. When we exercise this ability, we license the behavior. It doesn't make it right.

Here we must tread lightly.

In a well ordered society, central government would be too weak to have any influence over license. In a disordered society, central government issues licenses. America is highly disordered.

Government license is license. It is not right. Government cannot grant rights; it has none to give. Governments simply refrain from interfering with the rights God gave humanity. That's enough. The fact that people put so much credence in the moral authority of government proves that our society is disordered. Acceptances of deviant behavior must come from every man and woman, not government. If men and women refuse their consent, then the behavior remains deviant. And there's nothing government can do to change that.

As conservatives, we have a duty to preserve the things that work in society and to allow the things that don't work to die of loneliness. License needs to die. The trick is to stop using it.

How many times a day do you look for a problem? Many more than you realize. We are conditioned and genetically geared to look for danger. The problem is that we are also wired to find what we look for.

When self-help experts tell us to think about becoming rich, they teach us to rely on the mind's ability to find what it seeks.

"Seek and you shall find."

"The truth is out there, Scully."

So where do we look to see not license, but its opposite?

First, we look at ourselves. Pull out a notebook or open a text document on your computer and begin listing the times you refused to make excuses for yourself. When have you done something that deserved a consequence—however small—for which you accepted the consequence. This doesn't have to be a major sin or crime. It could be as simple as a hangover after a party or doing dishes in the morning because you were too lazy to do them after dinner.

Make the list as long as you can. Shoot for twenty times you've taken your medicine. If that's too easy, go for one hundred.

Next, look at others and do the same for them. This second list could include a spouse, children, friends, siblings, co-workers, and bosses--anyone you've spent time with. Look only for times these people stepped up and accepted consequences without sniveling or evading.

Then think about little ways to reward this behavior. Reward yourself. Send a note to one of the people on your other list, too. Say, "I want to let you know how proud I am of you—and impressed, frankly—that you had the courage to accept . . ." whatever it was they accepted. Don't mention the shortcoming, only the courage to accept the result.

Get into this habit of recognizing what works. For 30 days commit yourself to recognizing at least one act of accountability. If you can find examples of this accountability only in yourself, that's okay, but strive to recognize accountability in others. By "recognize," I mean rewarding the behavior.

You might wonder what good this recognition could do: "How can one person recognizing responsibility and reason once-a-day change society?" Because of three little possibilities:

1. Recognizing the desired behavior instead of criticizing the negative licentious behavior frees conservatives from the title "judgers." Like all good conservatives, I recognize that judging is important and valuable to individuals and societies. It's also impossible to avoid. We must judge and decide many, many times every day. When I look at my blog posts, though, I see that I spend far more time negatively describing things that I don't want and little time extolling the virtues of things I do want.

By shifting our focus from the wrong things to the right things, we're taking from our enemies a bludgeon they've long used against us. We've taken away the "judgmental" title. We'll judge just as much and just as severely, but we'll praise and reward the good things more often and criticize bad things less often. By this method, conservatism becomes a solution provider, not a problem finder.

2. There's no need to confine our habit to our little circles of friends. If you have a blog, write one blog post sometime in the next 30 days praising someone who took

responsibility for his actions. Repeat this step at least once a month.

If you don't have a blog, expand your recognition pattern beyond your intimate associations. Tell a stranger. Write a letter to the editor or to a member of Congress. How many letters of praise do you think the average state or federal legislator gets? I bet the number is less than 1 percent of their total constituent correspondence. You know that some staffer screens out most of the negative letters, but you can rest assured those staffers make sure the boss gets the positive messages. Since politicians are people, they'll eventually begin to give us more of what we praise and less of what we criticize.

3. If everyone you know has a copy of "Zen Conservatism," there will be many, many people rewarding anti-licentious behavior. If 100,000 people read this book and develop this habit, in one year they will recognize and reward 36.5 million courageous acts. If 1 million people read this book, one act of responsibility will be recognized for every person in America. Pretty quickly, acknowledging good behavior becomes the norm instead of the exception. (By the way, over 1 million people attended a Tea Party on April 15, 2009.)

Distraction

Distraction is License's ugly cousin and co-conspirator. Distraction is the abandonment of contemplation, the avoidance of serious thinking or profound action. Distraction tells us to turn away from anything we deem unpleasant until we spin in place unable to focus even on the gun pointed with laser-precision at our left temple.

Distraction is the opiate of the people, allowing them to see nothing despite their eyes and hear nothing despite their ears.

Distraction is 24-hour news that destroys faith in the viewer's hero for the sake of ratings.

Distraction is the gossip web site where sad people click and look and scan the pithy headlines disparaging a celebrity whose bad decisions left her open to ridicule before her comeback tour earns her millions from the sad people who once ridiculed her.

Distraction is the philosophy class that eats away the best years of a young woman's life as she perseverates over questions whose answers don't mean enough to change the direction of a water bug on the kitchen floor.

The perfectly distracted individual sees the world and life as the text on the label of a spinning 78 RPM record. (Kids, ask your grandparents.)

The opposite of distraction is focus, but focus can be misguided, too. Islamo-fascists are focused on terror. Ted Bundy was focused on murdering women. Child molesters are focused on destroying children. Yet each of these forces of evil believes his cause is worthy, that his focus is just. So how do we form focus?

The answer is God and on the beauty He gives us. Focus on God and you'll know where to focus. He is the way, the truth, and the life, and His truth will set us free.

If that's enough of an answer for you, try this: focus on a white wall. Pretend it's a movie screen. See the old numbers counting down to start the flick: eight - seven - six - five - four . . . Now on the screen see the sun peeking over the horizon miles away. Feel the rays of light caressing your face and scalp with warmth and love. Smell the newness of the day as the sun ignites the air with life and lightness. Now, say to yourself softly, "I see Him."

Your focus is set for the day. You've just experienced magic . . . the magic of the Constitutional Convention and of the signing of the Declaration of Independence. You've just felt what the people of

Boston felt when they gathered in the street beneath the balcony of the Old State House to hear Colonel Thomas Crafts read the Declaration for the first time.

Want more? If you get the chance, go to Boston and take the tour of the Old State House. Watch the movie first. Then go upstairs and take your turn standing on the tiny balcony. Tell me your knees don't quiver. Focus on that feeling, for that's God's vibration in your bones telling you, "they got it right."

Our focus on man-made things led to the financial crisis. Focus on things of man lead us, finally, to distraction. We seek truth in the objects of our focus. Finding none, we shift our focus. We become increasingly adept at recognizing things that lack truth, so our attention span shrinks until, again, we find ourselves staring at the label of the spinning 78 rpm record.

Distraction often works in concert with License. A classic example of people using Distraction to achieve License was the post-election attacks on Mormons in California. Proposition 8 was an amendment to the California state Constitution defining marriage as a permanent union between a man and a woman. It passed in November 2008, touching off violent and hysterical demonstrations and riots by opponents.

The gay rights activists who orchestrated the civil disobedience singled out Mormons for ridicule, accusation, and attack.

Like the Dreyfus affair in 19th century France, blaming Mormons for the majority view was a canard. It was a distraction. It was scapegoating and religious intolerance of the highest order.

But Proposition 8 opponents are distracting themselves. They are distracting themselves from the cold, biting reality that their neighbors and friends simply believe that marriage is not a legal state but a moral one. The state's laws, the majority believes, should reflect the moral reality of marriage. That's not hatred—that's mere faith.

Making this rebuke even more powerful is the fact that these disapproving folks show remarkable tolerance and love for their accusers and attackers within the militant gay rights establishment. Proposition 8's supporters, the majority, did not attack gays. They did not vilify or condemn their gay neighbors. They simply said, "I will not endorse your marriage. I will not grant the license you request."

When rebuke comes from someone demonstrably mean and nasty, it's easy to take. Consider the source. When rebuke comes from someone who loves us, it hurts.

The rebuke of gay marriage in California came from loving people. Ouch.

Complexity

> *Beauty is the ultimate defense against complexity.*
> David Gelentner

A few years ago I bought a book titled "Complexity" on a whim. I shouldn't have enriched the authors.

The book's mission was to convince readers that the world had become too complex to continue allowing people to choose. Instead, the co-authors opined, Harvard-educated experts must make all major decisions: which products come to market, which protocols and standards win, how much merchandise costs, even which styles of clothing are available each season. You see, these authors--all highly educated, award-winning scientists--believe that we've been getting it wrong for about 100 years. We elect the wrong presidents, we buy the wrong video tapes, we subscribe to the wrong magazines, and we marry the wrong mates.

Those authors don't reply to my simple emails asking them how Harvard and Oxford grads like

Franklin Raines, Jim Johnson, George W. Bush, Ben Bernanke, and Hank Paulson managed to destroy the US economy. Weren't these precisely the kinds of men required to deal modern complexity?

The authors, of course, were wrong. In fact, they were 180 degrees out. The problems we face today stem largely from too many people trusting the highly educated graduates of elite universities and distrusting the gut instincts of Joe the Plumber.

Complexity requires avoidance, not a Ph.D. Scientists embrace complexity even though it proves the bane of their existences. The pursuit of M-theory--string theory's next generation--drives some of the smartest minds on the planet to brink of insanity. From the Grand Unified Theory that Stephen Hawking wrote of in "A Brief History of Time" some 30 years ago, theoretical physics and mathematics have arrived only one step closer.

In three decades, the smartest mathematicians with the fastest, most powerful computers, with legions of adoring grad students to pursue every whim of possibility, have run into the same problem that science has met for 5,000 years: +1.

String theory postulated that everything was connected by a string of something. Not energy, because energy was one of the things on the string. More like a string of numbers. For a while, string theory was the answer to everything physicists could imagine, save one troubling problem: it worked better if there were two. A few brilliant scientists took string theory further: all the way to 11 "things." At this point, the numbers fell together so beautifully that all of theoretical physics believed the only steps remaining were to sweep the floor of the lab and take out the trash.

Except . . . plus one works better.

Either sweeping the floor or carrying the garbage to the alley, someone noticed a P-brane lying about and added it to the mix. P-branes are sort of like membranes without the mem- but with many dimensions represented by the letter P.

Look up P-branes, M-theory, string theory, or theoretical physics on Wikipedia and you'll soon see the same pattern that my little P-brane sees: the last theory is always one short of the last theory. Just as inspection of the atom revealed electrons and protons and neutrons which were made of quarks were made of other stuff and so on, the search for the beginning of time and the edge of the universe always finds just one more thing larger, older, or beyond.

Complexity is a tool of the wannabe Masters of the Universe. These Masters tell us that technology or economics or climate change or finance is just too complex for mere mortals to understand. "Let us worry about it," they say. "You just do the work and pay your taxes. We know best how to spend money."

Don't buy it for an instant. Complexity is a state of mind. Seek beauty and complexity disappears. Look upon the white field after nature has blanketed your world with snow, and you'll see beauty in the simplicity of a single color—or lack thereof. Look at the ocean on a sunny day and revel in the beauty in shades of blue. Bacon frying, coffee brewing, setting up a Christmas tree are all invitations to experience beauty through your nose. Watch a sunrise and picture angels shining a spotlight to see you better.

Complexity is man's attempt to shatter magic, while magic is the thing that makes babies happier than grown-ups. Babies believe in magic; grown-ups realize that it's all very complex. Babies seek truth and find it; grown-ups seek facts and are never satisfied. Babies thrill at the sight of a puppy; grown-ups make sure it doesn't pee on the carpet.

Babies live amid beauty and thereby become beauty itself; grown-ups complicate everything and thereby become complexity itself. If beauty is the ultimate defense against complexity, then it stands to reason that total complexity is the absence of beauty.

Make beautiful things, and complexity won't stand a chance.

What to Give Up

If you agree that conservatism staggers under the tonnage of too much stuff, follow me now to some solutions. I know from experience in business that letting go of the unnecessary is more difficult than taking on something new. That's why we have so much crap around us. Have you ever tried to clean out your closet? Have you ever tried to throw away the stuff you don't need from your basement?

The crap in our political attic remains out of nostalgia, sentiment, and emotion. We love it. We honor and revere our heritage. We miss Ronald Reagan and William F. Buckley. We long for the 1980s. Well and good. We should never let loose of those memories, those lessons.

But those men and moments were not the magic of the movement. We can honor Reagan without unearthing his body. We can study Buckley without buying the Suzy Wong[1]. We can preach Burke without wearing his jacket. Lately, it seems, we've been more

---

[1] Suzy Wong was the name of one of Buckley's favorite sailboats. Read "Atlantic High" by Wm. F. Buckley Jr. for more.

interested in festooning ourselves with the sentiment of conservatism than in whittling down the message to its essentials.

If Reagan, Buckley, and Burke spoke the truth, what forces could stand against them?

Sometimes in court, your best friend is your worst witness. He tries too hard. He dallies with perjury or exaggeration. He wants you to prevail so much that the opposing counsel turns him upside-down.

In the battle of the individual against the collective, we, the friends of the individual, may have tried too hard. We may have taken on too much of the burden of victory.

What's wrong with the Republican party? Lots.

The Republican Party

The GOP has been home to conservatism for longer than I can remember. But it felt funny, like we were a widowed aunt taken in by a reluctant niece. I'm not saying we should turn against the Republican party or form our own conservative party: either would likely weaken us. I am saying we need to treat the GOP like a vendor and not like an overlord.

The GOP sells election stuff to the highest bidder, and you bid with headcount. That's what all political parties do, so I'm not saying the RNC is any worse than the Democrats. If 20 million Americans decided tomorrow that the number one issue on which they will not compromise is crabgrass prevention, both parties will abandon every plank, platform, and principle expressed over the past 230 years of electioneering to become known as the Pre-emergent Party.

The only difference between the parties' approaches to the anti-crabgrass movement would be that the GOP would promote candidates with lawn care experience, while the Democrats would push candidates with backgrounds in organic farming.

Jason Lewis, filling in for Rush Limbaugh, described the problem perfectly in December 2008. He said that the problem conservatives face is that the Republican party measures election wins and losses, not liberation. The three kinds of seats up for election in 1980 were the White House, the Senate, and the House of Representatives. Democrats won 3 dozen more elections for these seats than Republicans.

Yet freedom advanced as a result. For the first time since Calvin Coolidge, Americans were freer in 1984 than they were in 1980. For four years, we progressed. For four years America measured proposed changes against Michael Novak's ultimate question: "Will it liberate."

I'll do the GOP the same favor that Jefferson did King George: I'll itemize our grievances so they can clean up their act before another colony jumps ship.

First, the GOP is *still* a party dominated by blue-blood, aristocratic statists from prep schools in states that have no ending "Rs". Conservatism never really felt at home there. For instance, William F. Buckley's father moved the family to *Mexico* to teach them conservatism away from the corrupting influence of Connecticut in the 1920s. Yet the GOP cannot win unless conservatives believe the Republican candidate is significantly more conservative than the Democrat.

Second, the people in charge of the GOP—namely the Chairmen—have run the party as if it were a business. It is not. The purpose of a business is to maximize returns to its owners. The purpose of a political party is to advance the core beliefs of significant percentage of the population. Its okay for the GOP lose money and races. It's not okay for the GOP to lose free market capitalism, fiscal restraint, defense spending, law and order, the House, the Senate, the White House, and 13 state legislatures in 2 elections.

Third, the Republican party is gentlemanly and ladylike. Politics ain't. The only time in my life when the GOP acted like Democrats was after the 2000 election. Hundreds of Republicans swarmed on Dade County,

Florida, to intimidate the Democrat intimidators who descended on Florida like locusts. It was a beautiful thing to see protesters who wore Brooks Brothers' suits and drank Heineken shouting down hippies in Che t-shirts and hemp belts holding up their Goodwill jeans. The bad news is, of course, those weren't real Republicans -- they were conservatives taking up the fight while Republicans watched CNN in their New York offices.

Fourth, the GOP has some serious fence mending to do with the right. Bob Dole sold us out with a tax increase in 1982 and on the Telecommunications Reform Act of 1996. Trent Lott sold us out by sharing power with Democrats in the Senate in 2001. Numerous House and Senate GOP leaders sold us out by . . . selling out to high bidders, also known as donors. George Bush sold us out repeatedly. I could name a hundred other back-stabbing, weasel-kneed sell-outs by senior Republican officials, but I'll spare you the blood pressure spike. Instead, I'll rest my case on a single word: TARP.

The GOP usurps and distorts conservatism for its own purposes, then blames conservatism when the party's ham-fisted attempts at presidential politics blow up in their Ivy League faces, undoing thousands of dollars worth of orthodontics. This annoying habit deserves a look.

Borrowing a stupid idea from his father, George W. Bush ran his 2000 presidential campaign on the concept of "compassionate" conservatism. Compassionate conservatism is actually liberalism with low taxes. But the real problem I have is with the term itself.

If George W. Bush were a "compassionate" conservative, what kind am I? What kind was Ronald Reagan?

Remember George H. W. Bush's campaign theme in 1988? "A kinder, gentler conservatism?" The only difference between the two Bush's was the number of middle initials. After 8 years of the greatest president of the 20th century, Bush 41's theme can only be a repudiation of Reagan's presidency as unkind and too rough. How ungrateful to the man (and his admirers) who rescued George H. W. Bush's Republican party from the cesspool of Watergate.

Conservatism must not allow the GOP to take us for granted. The RNC cannot count on our support simply because the Republican candidate is not a Democrat. Either *we* run the Republican National Committee like a party on the right, or the Republican party must align itself to our agenda. The days of propping up conservative imitators are over.

Here are the essential behaviors in dealing with a political party:

Conservatives call themselves conservatives not Republicans, just as actors call themselves actors and not "Hamlet." Conservative is what we are; Republican is the party we bring to life now and then.

Conservatives make parties earn their donations. "Do you want Barack Obama to exhume and desecrate Mother Teresa's body? We need your help to stop him." Sure, I shattered computer keyboards tapping out an electronic payment to McCain-Palin every time Obama promised to give more of my money to some flea-bag moocher in a moo-moo. That doesn't make it smart. Instead of bucks for anyone with an elephant on his lapel, why not show me how my $50 will elect a House candidate who wrote her master's thesis on saving the planet with the 10th Amendment?

Conservatives put the party first when the party deserves it, and raise hell when the party goes wobbly. When Ronald Reagan ran for president in 1980, conservatives got out the vote, beginning with their friends and neighbors. Jamie McGauley, who sat in front of me in Biology, told me in 1979 that I needed to learn more about Ronald Reagan. I did and jumped on the bandwagon with both feet. When the party leads, we ensure victory.

Conservatives know their principles better than the issues. There's really no such thing as an issues voter. No one voted for Barack Obama because of his stance on an issue. They couldn't have, because he didn't take a stance on anything. They voted for his theme. We voted for Reagan because of his principles. Smart politicians leave it to the electorate to apply their themes to real issues.

Conservatives demand resoluteness and steadfastness from their party. A former boss of mine told me that, while he disagrees with everything George W. Bush stands for, he admires the fact that he knows how to stick to a plan. Our plan is 230 years old, embodied in the Declaration, the Constitution, and the Bill of Rights. We'll work ourselves to death for a party that sticks to *that* plan.

Conservatives concentrate their capital on the essentials. This means we don't need a four hundred page wish list of Republican goals vetted through 72 focus groups and standardized across 97 tracking polls in 238 demographic/psychograhpic groups in 132 micro-regions from sea to shining sea. It means that we know four things you better never compromise: Life, Liberty, the Pursuit of Happiness, and Enumerated Powers of government.

Conservatives will chair the meeting; a seat at the table is not sufficient. We have slowly fallen for the idiotic and corrupt UN mentality when it comes to policy and principle: as long as everyone gets a chance to speak, no one can complain with the oligarchy's decision to triple taxes on beer, wine, and spirits. So long as our society equates good conversation with good government, then conservatives will *be* the Republican party's oligarchy—or we don't play.

The essential lesson here is that conservatism is not a political party. We employ political parties to advance our "tacit acknowledgment that all things finally important to the human experience are behind us," as Buckley said.

The Religious Right

The Religious Right remains a powerful force within conservatism. But it, too, has lost focus. A large number of evangelicals swoon to the siren songs of man-made global warming. Many others attempt to apply Christian doctrine to government in ways that just don't work. For instance, we are each obliged to help the poor, feed the hungry, and clothe the naked. Government is not. And government poverty programs do not relieve any individual of his duties in these areas. You can't tell Jesus, "I didn't feed you when you were hungry because you should have applied for food stamps."

So why should we jettison this enormous voting block that helped put Reagan and George H. W. Bush into the White House?

Because the Christian Right just isn't what it used to be. And the factors that required a strong religiosity in national public life have changed since 1980.

Don't read too much into this. I believe that Judeo-Christian faith and values do and must always underlie all decision making: personal, economic, governmental, and voting booth. Without a strong foundation in Judeo-Christian values, no person will make grounded decisions. Instead, "situational ethics" will prevail which means any horror is okay so long as it's effectively justified.

The Religious Right, though, must be held in check. The Founders envisioned a national government constrained—"chained" according to my friend Paul Curtman—by the Constitution. Delegates to the Constitutional Convention saw their product as a license that permitted government to perform seventeen activities, for which Congress was authorized to lay and collect taxes uniformly from the states based on population. That's it.

The Founders, to the best of my knowledge, never intended that US government would involve itself in matters like abortion or birth control, homosexual or heterosexual marriage, or myriad other issues that both the left and the Christian Right would like Washington to manage. The founders expected that the states would deal with such matters, if governments needed to deal with them at all. The founders, I'm sure, assumed that wise and honest federal judges and justices would, if presented such cases, refuse to hear the matters on the grounds of jurisdiction. As Robert Bork pointed out, these are political matter, first off, not judicial matters. Second, they belong to the states. Were Congress to overreach and pass laws regarding abortion, the Supreme Court should strike the laws down since the Constitution is mute.

I agree that abortion is an abomination on par with slavery. I do not agree that the solution is to ignore the rule of law by making federal laws that prohibit abortion.

In Robert Bolt's timeless play, "A Man For All Seasons," Thomas More argues with his son-in-law, Will Roper. Roper wants More to arrest all who violate laws of morality. When More informs Roper he'd give even the Devil the benefit of the law, Roper says he'd cut

down every law in the land to get at the Devil. More's reply:

Oh? And when the last law was down, and the Devil turned round on you, where would you hide, Roper, the laws all being flat? This country's planted thick with laws from coast to coast -- man's laws, not God's -- and if you cut them down -- and you're just the man to do it -- do you really think you could stand upright in the winds that would blow then? Yes, I'd give the Devil benefit of law, for my own safety's sake.

Well, that's a better argument than I could ever develop for sticking to the rule of law. If we want the government confined to enumerated powers when it suits us, then we live with the results when it doesn't. The solution to abortion is prayer and better Supreme Court justices. When the time is right and the court is honest, a case will present itself that compels the jurists to expose Roe v. Wade for the fraud it was. The matter will return to the states, or to the people, where it belongs.

I love the Christian Right. In many ways, I am one. Like Roe v. Wade, I believe McCollum v. Board of Education was a travesty. This matter, I believe, is easily fixed with a Constitutional Amendment, but I wouldn't lead off with that in my campaign because it will cost the election. Trust me. The focus must be on limiting the government to its Constitutional duties. Once that's done—and the people are comfortable with smaller government—we can turn our attention to anti-religious and anti-life rulings from the Supreme Court. But first focus on the simple things: the rule of law.

Am I saying we should kick out or ridicule the Religious Right? Absolutely not. In fact, I believe we should be tightly bound to them. We have much in common. Our differences, for the post part, are in priorities. But our coalition runs from Religious Right to the Libertarians, and we need them all. What we *don't* need is Rinos. Everyone else is welcome.

Political Organizations, Think Tanks and other conservative causes that rely on donations have increased hundreds-fold over the past 30 years. You cannot participate in or donate to all of them. The very existence of so many redundant causes dilutes the effectiveness and energy of conservatism. In chapter # we'll look at ways to cull the herd, allowing some of these committees and and causes to fail to that what remains is stronger and more effective.

For two weeks after the 2008 election, I counted every request for a donations I received in the mail. In 12 mail-delivery days, I received 28 solicitations from 15 different organizations. Each asked for a minimum donation of $25. In other words, theoretically conservative organizations asked me for at least $9,750 a year in donations.

The problem is not really the dollar amount. It's the dilution. It's the lack of focus. It's the sheer number of things that want my attention, money, time, and energy.

Once upon a time, conservatives had very few outlets for their political action money. Let's go back to 1980. We had Young Americans for Freedom, the Heritage Foundation, the Stanford Institute, the Christian Coalition, Birthright, the National Right to Life Association, the National Taxpayers Union, and the National Rifle Association, the National Right to Work, and a few others.

Among periodicals, we had National Review, Reason, The American Spectator, and a few quarterlies from the Heritage Foundation.

In 1980, our message, our energies, our money, and our efforts were *focused*. And we won consistently from 1980 through 1988.

Today, Wikipedia lists 135 conservative organizations in the United States and the list is growing so fast they admit they can't keep up. Today, we are unfocused. Each of the 135 organizations listed struggles for money from a donor pool only about 8 percent larger than it was in 1980.

Take a few moments to go to your computer and navigate to Wikipedia. Search for "Conservative Organizations."

Start with the As and read the various organizations' charters and purposes. Notice the redundancies. Each is for "sound government." Each is for "limited government." Each "advances conservative principles." But do we really need 135 organizations doing the same thing?

There's something called The Adam Smith Foundation founded in 1997. While we all love and admire Adam Smith and we all wish more people would read P. J. O'Rourke's wonderful examination of "The Wealth of Nations," this Adam Smith Foundation seems very confused about Adam Smith. It's primary mission, it seems, is to change Missouri's method of appointing judges. I have read "The Wealth of Nations," and I'm pretty sure Smith never discussed the right way to appoint judges to state courts in Missouri.

Americans for Honesty in Government was founded 2006, apparently to allow its members to distinguish themselves from the millions of Americans who want dishonesty in government, a la Chicago, Illinois.

When we dilute our political action donations among 134 or 350 organizations, we dilute our influence, as well. Do we need *that* many conservative clubs and organizations? There weren't that many in the late 1970s, yet we managed to elect Reagan and a Congress that was conservative enough to pass all of Reagan's major initiatives. That success inspired well-meaning people to launch a whole bunch of new organizations. Perhaps if we concentrated our efforts into a couple dozen of the best groups, those groups would become more effective and our political action dollars would have a greater impact.

Later in the book, you'll learn several ways to make your dollars more effective.

Blogs, News, and Web Sites

Blogs and Web Sites didn't exist when we elected Reagan. When we took back the House and Senate in 1994, only a handful of conservative forums existed on the internet. I wrote for Town Hall forum on CompuServe and participated in a few forums on America Online. The proliferation of conservative blogs and websites has diluted the impact of the best. No one has time to read all of them every day. Chapter # suggests ways conservatives can raise many voices effectively without diluting our message or overwhelming our audiences.

The top 10 most popular blogs according to Technorati in January 2009 included two statist blogs (Huffington Post and Daily Kos) but not a single conservative blog. In fact, more half a dozen statist blogs rank higher than the top conservative blog, www.michellemalkin.com.

One could make the argument that conservative blogs rank low because statists significantly out number conservatives. I won't buy that. Rather, I think there are simply too many good conservative blogs. Readership is diluted.

Moreover, on any given day, the conservative blogs on my blogroll contain slightly different takes on the same 3 or 4 news stories: global warming insanity, Democrat scandals, proliferation of government, and the economy.

This diluted readership also dilutes our message. Conservatives know where to find content they want, but the less politically conscious who are simply looking for information tend to go to the top ranked blogs. This is a classic case of the rich getting richer, only here it's the Technorati authority of the left's blogs that accumulate ever more readers.

Conservatives would be well advised to organize their blogging a bit more intelligently.

One option would be to specialize. Tom Nelson and Anthony Watts run fantastic blogs on climate and only on climate. Tom digests the AGW news of the day with quick quips on each story that allows readers to get all their news in one, quick look. Anthony Watts, a seasoned meteorologist, provides deep dives into particular aspects of global warming from a scientist's point of view.

By focusing both their subjects and their style, Tom and Anthony blow away most other AGW skeptic sites. Readers know where to go to get what they need. Serious research can begin (and sometimes end) with WattsUpWithThat.com. You can satisfy your casual curiosity at tomnelson.blogspot.com. Links from both sites take you to more in-depth information you might want or need.

There are other focused conservative blogs. Several conservatives focus on economics. During the entertaining downfall of faux American Indian professor Ward Churchill, Jonathan Paine maintained The Pirate Ballerina (www.pirateballerina.com) focused on the mad professor. It remains a study of great single-subject blogging.

Another emerging trend is the aggregated blog. A few years ago, several liberty-focused blogs in Colorado formed the The People's Press Collective (www.peoplespresscollective.com). This blog consolidates a dozen center-right blogs in one package. The result is a news team that fills the void created when the mainstream media turned themselves into shills for big government.

The success of this model could have a major impact on freedom. It could also contribute to zen conservatism. You, the news consumer, can start your day with your local press collective's blog. There you'll find links to major stories about government corruption, freedom, and taxes, divided into national and local departments. This model freezes out the leftist propaganda by giving citizen journalists a unified forum without imposing restrictive editorial policies on any writer.

In the St. Louis area, several bloggers and organizations have started www.minutemanblog.org based on the Colorado model. As this book goes to press, the site is in beta testing. When it launches, readers will have easy, one-stop shopping for important news from their favorite bloggers.

Meetings

Conservatives and Republicans tend toward organization. We apply things we see at work to political action. Sometimes, a well crafted reporting hierarchy helps accomplish complex goals, sort through competing opportunities, and sustain a movement through rough times. Most of the time, though, complex organization gets in the way.

As the St. Louis Tea Party movement became more successful, the many small clubs and groups that comprise a large part of the movement wanted to build a more organized structure. These groups began looking at the org charts of political action committees, companies, and even political parities for guidance.

In one week, I spent over 4 hours talking and meeting about building this big organization. Then, thankfully, Dana Loesch slapped some sense into me.

I work 50 hours a week to make a living and another 50 hours a week on the tea party movement. Every minute I spend organizing and meeting about organizing is a minute I'm not advancing the American Revolution or disrupting the enemy's battle plans.

If conservatives and libertarians want the American Revolution to continue, they better spend a lot less time in meetings and a lot more time on the streets.

John McCain, Bob Dole, and George H. W. Bush didn't lose elections because of too few meetings; they lost because of too little action.

Like me, most conservative political activists have full time jobs outside of politics. Many have jobs that require more than 40 hour work weeks. We squeeze our revolution into evenings, weekends, and lunch breaks.

Working 50 hours a week for a paycheck and 50 hours a week to save the republic requires discipline to avoid over-organization.

But . . .

There is one thing we will not give up: Power! We will make as our credo William F. Buckley's rant in "Up From Liberalism":

> I will not cede more power to the state. I will not willingly cede more power to anyone, not to the state, not to General Motors, not to the CIO. I will hoard my power like a miser, resisting every effort to drain it away from me. I will then use my power, as I see fit. I mean to live my life an obedient man, but obedient to God, subservient to the wisdom of my ancestors; never to the authority of political truths arrived at yesterday at the voting booth. That is a program of sorts, is it not? It is certainly program enough to keep conservatives busy, and Statists at bay. And the nation free.

So shall we hoard power. But we will first recover the power usurped by Congress, courts, and Presidents over the past 70 years. We gladly give up the silly material toys of distraction, license, and complexity if we must. We will fill the void in our lives with the power God gave us as human beings. We will steal it away from the thieving politicians and judges who stole it from us, not only at the ballot box, but through anti-Constitutional an un-American court rulings.

When Buckley wrote "Up From Liberalism," he possessed orders-of-magnitude more personal power and liberty than we do today. And we, today, hold more power than we will tomorrow. The Government has been like a siphon, first requiring outside mechanical force, but then relying only on gravity to pull our power from our souls, to bleed dry our bank accounts, to drain our liberty. So yelling "Stop!" no longer suffices. We must yell,

"Give it BACK!"

Focus on One Goal

Napoleon mastered the art of illusion. He used feints and small, rapid attacks to make his enemy feel surrounded. Unable to see the battle from above, the enemy became convinced that all hope for victory was lost. Soon the opposing general worried only about survival, about escaping with as many men and supplies as he could salvage.

The statists employ the same tactics to achieve their goals. During the first 100 days of his administration, Obama announced major, new initiatives up to three times a week. The initiatives were usually unrelated: releasing terrorists from Guantanamo Bay one day, healthcare socialization the next, then expanded access to free and easy abortions.

Obama's goal was to get conservatives chasing their tails. By changing the main story, opposition response was lost in the next day's news cycle. Conservatives would look like reactionaries, simply opposing one initiative after another.

There are pro-life organizations, states' rights organizations, libertarian organizations that focus on reduced government, Second Amendment, First Amendment, and religious freedom organizations. Each of these groups plays a critical role in offering America a future even greater than its past. But all of these groups will fail if they let the statist President set the agenda.

For the first 60 days of the Tea Party movement, focus was absolute. First was February 27 with its theme of "Repeal the pork, or retire." Immediately, the movement went to work on the Tax Day protests which drew over 1.2 million Americans into parks, streets, and stadiums in 900 cities across all 50 states. Our focus was so keen that Barack Obama felt compelled to mock our patriotism and ambition.

When the President offered to meet with the Tea Party organizers and have "a serious dialogue," we responded immediately with hand-delivered acceptance to meet in St. Louis, Missouri, for a live, televised forum. The White House blinked.

If we avoid the temptation to fight every battle, to respond to every event, to answer every challenge, we will lose. So choose your passion. And choose wisely.

Abortion is a terrible sin that stains our nation with the blood of innocents. We cannot stop it while pro-abortionists control the White House, both houses of Congress, and the Supreme Court. We must first win the political battle by electing a conservative Congress with a Senate majority that will block the appointment of judges who legislate from the bench.

The right to keep and bear arms is central to a republic's survival. We cannot guarantee or extend that right while statists control the White House, both houses of Congress, and the courts. When we take control of Congress, we can block any attempt to limit gun ownership and roll back any laws intended to make the manufacture and sale of guns and ammunition too expensive.

Freedom of speech, assembly, and the press are germane to liberty, and the statists hope to eliminate all three. We cannot stop them except through massive victories at the ballot box. These victories will be all the more difficult as the White House, both houses of Congress, and the courts conspire to eliminate dissenting opinions by labeling them "hate crimes." We must first win back the Congress, and then legislate away the curbs on our liberties.

You see the pattern here: conservative social, economic, judicial, and moral objectives are in danger of obliteration unless we change Congress and keep it changed. Asking statists to change their minds is a fool's game. Instead, we must replace them with conservative alternatives—men and women who understand the limits of the federal government as expressed in the Constitution; men and women who are bold enough to eliminate every federal law, program, and department not specifically required by Article 1, Section 8 of the Constitution.

In his book "The Power of Less," author Leo Babauta gives for simple principles for achieving focus:

Focus on a Goal

Focus on Now

Focus on the Task at Hand

Focus on the Positive

I find Leo's method remarkably simple and effective. Let's borrow his focus list.

Create a Focus Card

Begin each day by writing one or two sentences for each of these 4 focus areas. You might want to file these cards away as a history of your contribution to restoring the republic. If you wish—and I recommend you do— make one card for each area of your life: work, family, faith, finances, fitness, etc. But, at the very least, do it for the noble cause of the republic. Here's an example:

> Goal: A conservative majority in both houses of Congress following 2010 election.
>
> Now Focus: Hold a house party next week to begin selecting a conservative candidate from each party to support in next year's senate race.
>
> Task at Hand Focus: Send 20 invitations to friends and neighbors.
>
> Positive Focus: Putting my energy into electing candidates I truly support.

By establishing one goal and writing it first, your mind will guide your actions toward its successful completion. If one million people follow this stratagem, we will complete 500 million positive steps toward the goal of a pro-liberty majority in Congress. With 500 million positive actions, we will prevail.

Keep a Journal or Log

On November 3, 2010, you will wake up to a new morning in America. The slide toward statism will have slowed dramatically by your actions leading up to Election Day. You'll want to reflect on what our country has been through. You'll want to remember what you did to pull us back from the brink.

Four years later, America will have moved toward freedom and away from despotism. You'll give your journal to a child or grandchild. "Here. Read what I did to restore this great republic for you."

While the fight for liberty and against statist tyranny will never end, momentum will change teams. Your journal will be a treasure trove of memories and lessons for the next generation. Record your battle so your posterity will have a guide, a family guide, to fighting back against the dark forces of totalitarianism.

Keep your journal on paper, if possible. Even if you'd prefer to use a blog or word processor, print the pages and bind them. Treasure the printed page and guard it with your life. Those who would take our liberty will take our papers, our memories, and shred them. They do not want your children to know the truth—that's why they've worked so hard to seize the schools. They do not want your grandchildren to know your story—that's they work to make America's past something evil.

Record the news of the day, the threats against our freedom, the national debt, the things the statists are doing to make that debt worse. Record your actions, the focuses on your 3 X 5 cards. Report on what worked and what didn't. Celebrate every little victory in writing for your children, and note the better ways we discover along the way.

Predict the Past

Futureme.org is a web site that sends emails at some future date, at least 90 days from the day you write it. We know from psychology and neuroscience that writing about a goal as if it's already happened causes the subconscious mind to work continuously toward that end. The subconscious doesn't like to be proven wrong. This means you can journal the future—predict the past, as it were.

Send yourself a note in the future. Go to www.futureme.org and send yourself four emails to be delivered at critical times:

Ninety days from today, tell yourself what you've accomplished in the interceding three months. Write it as if it's already happened, in the past tense. Be specific: "On July 4, 2009, I attended the 'Learn the Constitution' tea party and made three new friends."

One-hundred eighty days from today, telling yourself the specific things you did to recover some of the personal liberty you've lost to power-hungry politicians.

One year from today, tell yourself who you will help elect in the next general election.

Send yourself an email to arrive on November 4, the day after the general election. This email should congratulate you for the critical role you played in freedom's victory the day before. "We Won" makes a great subject line.

When you receive these emails, they'll delight you. But please don't limit your use of this powerful tool to just your political life. Future journaling will help you achieve any reasonable goal. Do you want to get an A in a class you're taking next semester? Then tap out a note to yourself tonight for delivery at the end of the semester: "I got an A in Trigonometry!"

Want to find your dream job? Try future journaling about your first day on the job as if you'd just gotten home from that first day. "By 3:00, I was exhausted, but I didn't know where the time went. It was better than I'd imagined."

While you could use an old fashioned pen and notebook, getting that email long after its writing had receded into your subconscious gives that future date great meaning. If you didn't achieve the goal, there's a good chance you'll be glad you didn't. If you did achieve it, or something close, you'll be inspired to journal your next future goal, starting the process over again.

The key to future journaling, though, is to write in the past tense, as if you've already achieved the goal. "I hope" is weak. "I did" is powerful. Remember, we want power.

Four Pillars of Conservatism

Life on earth is a temporary blessing

"In the time of your life, live - so that in that wondrous time you shall not add to the misery and sorrow of the world, but shall smile to the infinite variety and mystery of it." -- William Saroyan, The Time of Your Life

Of all the things conservatives conserve, life comes first. We defend life against threats; we celebrate life; we cherish life. The tragedy of abortion extends beyond the innocent baby killed to the mother, her parents, doctors, nurses, the aborted child's future siblings, the father, society, and the world. Such an enormous loss from such a tiny baby.

Perhaps the best way we can promote the values of life is to better celebrate life's joys and mysteries.

About a year ago, we adopted a little puppy from a different kind of shelter. This shelter isn't for strays, but for puppies from puppy mills. It seems that in our relentless pursuit of more, we've created quite a market for designer puppies. A cottage industry has sprung up to breed odd, cute hybrid dogs--like Yorkie-Poos.

Most of the little puppies in these litters are flawed in some way. Poor breeding and woeful conditions produce less-than-desirable animals. They are sick, ugly, or both. And in our society, the ugly must be killed. When the Human Society raided a rural Missouri puppy mill recently, it uncovered hundreds of puppy carcasses. The carcasses belonged to the ugly ones that wouldn't fetch $400 in a Mall pet shop. These ugly puppies were buried alive.

That's where this shelter comes in. Instead of rescuing inner city strays, this shelter rescues suburban and rural hybrids. They rescue the ugly ones destined for the gas chamber--or whatever economical instrument of death such puppy mills employ.

My wife doesn't agree, but our little Stella is an ugly dog. She looks like a black piñata with a few white hairs sprinkled randomly around her back.

I think about this dog when I'm driving home from work. I know that when the garage door starts to open, she'll stand and cock her head, concentrating at the mud room door. When I've parked in the garage, she'll be off the couch and sniffing under that door. When I open the door from the garage to the mud room, I'll hear her slapping the inner door. When I open the inner door, I'll see her dancing on hind legs, forepaws waving above her head.

For the next two minutes, she'll shower me with dance, licks, and bites. She'll end up in my arms like a baby, her head on my left shoulder, content to be carried throughout the house for as long as I should wish to carry her.

If this rescued puppy gives so much joy, how much greater is the joy in the reunion of a child and his father? How much sweeter is the sight of a baby's chin on her mommy's shoulder, drop of spit-up on her little, round chin?

We blur the vision of life's beauty. A puppy adjusts our lenses.

Take time to breathe in such moments when God's light brightens life itself. Celebrate life when it happens. Don't expect anything too fancy or elaborate—those things take planning, planning often subtracts from the moment. Celebrate life in its essence.

The next time you're in a store, look for a child. Listen to what she tells her parents. Don't even think about suppressing the smile you feel wash across your face when a two-year-old careful extends the index finger of left hand toward a box of cereal or a stuffed animal. That's life at its best, and the sooner you realize and accept it, the better off you'll be.

Don't worry about the germs on the box or on the little angel's finger. Just thank God He made her and that He spoke to you through her adorable actions.

Liberty is a gift from God to man

"Aye, fight and you may die. Run, and you'll live... at least a while. And dying in your beds, many years from now, would you be willin' to trade ALL the days, from this day to that, for one chance, just one chance, to come back here and tell our enemies that they may take our lives, but they'll never take... OUR FREEDOM!" -- *William Wallace*, Braveheart

When I first read Alexis de Tocqueville's "Democracy in America," the hair on my neck stood at attention like soldiers on a parade ground before some mighty dignitary. A palpable fear shook my psyche. Its reverberations echo in my heart and soul some 28 years later, the way some scientists claim the Big Bang can still be heard pin-balling around the universe.

I allowed myself a few days to digest the reality of last year's election. I needed only a second. Immediately of thought of Tocqueville's horrifying paragraphs on despotism in America.

It would seem that if despotism were to be established among the democratic nations of our days, it might assume a different character; it would be more extensive and more mild; it would degrade men without tormenting them.

Now, recall what Barack Obama told a Chicago Public Radio audience in the 1990s:

[I] think there was a tendency to lose track of the political and community organizing and activities on the ground that are able to put together the actual coalition of powers through which you bring about redistributive change

Tocqueville:

I think, then, that the species of oppression by which democratic nations are menaced is unlike anything that ever before existed in the world; our contemporaries will find no prototype of it in their memories.

Tocqueville on the pursuit of the petty:

The first thing that strikes the observation is an innumerable multitude of men, all equal and alike, incessantly endeavoring to procure the petty and paltry pleasures with which they glut their lives.

Tocqueville on isolation:

Each of them, living apart, is as a stranger to the fate of all the rest; his children and his private friends constitute to him the whole of mankind. As for the rest of his fellow citizens, he is close to them, but he does not see them; he touches them, but he does not feel them; he exists only in himself and for himself alone; and if his kindred still remain to him, he may be said at any rate to have lost his country.

And the most frightening paragraph ever written about America's future:

Above this race of men stands an immense and tutelary power, which takes upon itself alone to secure their gratifications and to watch over their fate. That power is absolute, minute, regular, provident, and mild. It would be like the authority of a parent if, like that authority, its object was to prepare men for manhood; but it seeks, on the contrary, to keep them in perpetual childhood: it is well content that the people should rejoice, provided they think of nothing but rejoicing. For their happiness such a government willingly labors, but it chooses to be the sole agent and the only arbiter of that happiness; it provides for their security, foresees and supplies their necessities, facilitates their pleasures, manages their principal concerns, directs their industry, regulates the descent of property, and subdivides their inheritances: what remains, but to spare them all the care of thinking and all the trouble of living?

Once again, look at Obama's vision for America. Look at his idea of change. Tell me if this doesn't sound like Obama wants for America what Tocqueville feared:

[T]he Constitution is a charter of negative liberties. Says what the states can't do to you. Says what the Federal government can't do to you, but doesn't say what the Federal government or State government must do on your behalf.

Sometimes it feels as if America lies battered and naked beneath the beast of government, this ideological rapist, this *ante partum* "mild despotism" that makes itself "the sole agent and only arbiter" of our happiness. We know the rapist will, barring some miracle, penetrate our sacred political virginity taking what was not offered, what is not his to take.

Until recently we chose not to fight but to live with the festering wounds inflicted by his desire to control us. We chose not to scream out but to quietly acquiesce to his unholy quest for pleasure.

Many of our fellow citizens long ago reached that state where they cede all power to the state. Peggy "the Moocher," as Michelle Malkin calls her, told Fox News that Obama would pay for her gasoline and mortgage so that she need never work again. Peggy would celebrate being spared "all the care of thinking and all the trouble of living." Peggy needs our help.

If you remember nothing else from this book, please remember this. Remember Tocqueville's 1838 prediction of what Obama's government would look like:

> It covers the surface of society with a network of small complicated rules, minute and uniform, through which the most original minds and the most energetic characters cannot penetrate, to rise above the crowd. The will of man is not shattered, but

softened, bent, and guided; men are seldom forced by it to act, but they are constantly restrained from acting. Such a power does not destroy, but it prevents existence; it does not tyrannize, but it compresses, enervates, extinguishes, and stupefies a people, till each nation is reduced to nothing better than a flock of timid and industrious animals, of which the government is the shepherd.

Well, *I am energetic, damn it*, and my mind is original--at least, I think so. Most of the people I know and admire, many who will disagree with everything I write, are energetic and original. How dare anyone stop us from rising above the crowd? We are not Peggy the Moocher! We are Americans, endowed by our Creator with certain unalienable rights, one of which is the pursuit of happiness. I, for one, would rather be dead than nonexistent. Wouldn't you?

Please read the entire chapter on Despotism in volume 4 of Democracy in America. You should know what's happening to you even if you lack the will and the fortitude to do anything about it. As Tocqueville warns:

It is indeed difficult to conceive how men who have entirely given up the habit of self-government should succeed in making a proper choice of those by whom they are to be governed; and no one will ever believe that a liberal, wise, and energetic government can spring from the suffrages of a subservient people

Let's not vilify Barack Obama for speaking his mind. In fact, we should thank him. He's been telling us for 20 years that he believes people are incapable of running their own lives.

Also remember that Obama did not elect himself; we did. Obama does not subject himself to the mild despotism of a gentle tyrant; we do. Instead, let's examine our own consciences.

Do we seek liberty or convenience?

Do we want more or better?

Do we trade freedom for cool new toys?

Do we look to Washington for happiness or social security?

Can you conceive of how a subservient people can produce a "wise, and energetic government?"

What Tocqueville tells us in that last paragraph is that the American notion of liberty, protected by its government in 1800, resulted not from Britain's tyranny over us, but by its lack. We were not oppressed as we claimed in the Declaration; we were free enough to crave freedom even more. Our form of government and social order sprang from free minds, because subservient people can conceive only of more favorable tyranny.

If we must be slaves, let's be slaves to God and to freedom, not to government. Let's chain ourselves to kind masters who trust us with the bolt-cutters. Let's wake up early and work hard at the labors that give us pleasure. Let's be wise enough to seek out labors that profit us by satisfying others. Let's free our minds from the tyranny of many shiny things. Let's secure our own safety as far as we can, granting government a license to protect us only from those monsters that we cannot battle on our own. Let us *earn* our Republic . . . and, this time, keep it.

Happiness is of our own making

> "For their happiness such a government willingly labors, but it chooses to be the sole agent and the only arbiter of that happiness" -- Alexis de Tocqueville, *Democracy in America*

Many religions advocate contemplation and meditation. In Roman Catholicism, meditation usually involves deep, internal consideration of prayers and revelations. For instance, Father John Corapi—arguably the greatest living Catholic preacher—speaks of spending an entire day meditating only a few words of the Ave Maria.

One flaw in modern American education which threatens to undermine the Founders' understanding of the proper relationship of man to government is the lack of serious meditation upon key phrases in our animating documents. So, how does one explain "the pursuit of happiness?"

Perhaps, one doesn't.

Instead, meditate on this: Why did Jefferson list "life" and "liberty" as absolutes, but use the phrase "pursuit of happiness?" Is it because happiness was never a guarantee? If not guaranteed, then something else could result, right?

So, in the Founders' eyes, God guaranteed man the right to pursue happiness, but not its acquisition. Think of a parent who permits his child to try out for the basketball team at school. While the parent promises to allow the child to pursue his or her dream of playing a game, the parent does not guarantee the child will make the team.

In fact, if the child were guaranteed a spot on the roster, there would be no pursuit. Guaranteed outcomes deny the right to pursue. One cannot pursue something one already possesses.

The guarantee of outcomes, then, is antithetical to a right we believe we are granted by God Almighty. When every kid on the baseball team gets a trophy, the pursuit of victory and excellence becomes meaningless. When every T-Ball game must end in a tie, the pursuit of victory becomes futile. When a car, a home, health insurance, and a hot, young wife are guaranteed by a paternalistic government, then pursuing those things becomes a waste of time. When incomes are guaranteed and identical, the pursuit of great ideas and excellent service become ridiculous wastes of time.

Guaranteeing the pursuit of happiness makes us free; guaranteeing happiness makes us irrelevant.

On the object of that pursuit, consider that Jefferson speaks of "happiness," while Locke (and the Virginia Charter) spoke of "property." This is an important distinction.

It seems that the Founders might have considered property a means rather than an end. To Jefferson, property was what you used to farm, to manufacture, to read and write, to earn a living and to subsist. Land and personal property were not guaranteed by God because a given person might come up short. One might pursue a large house in the suburbs but never acquire it.

Pursuing the property is guaranteed because you believe acquiring land will make you happy. No government may interfere with your pursuit of money, land, whatever object you desire, so long as you do not deprive another of his rightful property or liberty in the process. But neither may a government provide you with that object of your pursuit, for a government owns nothing but things confiscated from a person. Your right to pursue happiness ends it meets someone else's desire not to play. And the government has no moral authority to cross that line on your behalf.

Making Conservatism Attractive

Learn Emotional Advertising

During a 1966 interview with William F. Buckley Jr., Barry Goldwater said, "Fifty-five percent of the people are conservatives; they just don't know." Goldwater undercounted.

In the Battleground Poll conducted each presidential election cycle since 1984, question D3 asks respondents to describe their ideological bent. Every year since 1984, the numbers have varied only by one or two percentage points. Almost two-thirds of Americans describe themselves as Very Conservative or Somewhat Conservative. Only one-third call themselves Liberal (very or Somewhat). America is a conservative nation.

So why doesn't that ideological bent result in conservative wins at the ballot box? For several reasons:

- Only two conservatives, Barry Goldwater and Ronald Reagan, have won a party's nomination for President
- Voters tend to vote for the candidate of a party over ideology
- Conservative votes are split between the two parties or among several "third" parties

- Many people who describe themselves as conservative do not understand the ideological bent of candidates

To me, these points add up to political clutter. Political clutter is like house clutter—stuff we don't really need, but we're too lazy or to oblivious to pitch it out. If we don't pitch it out, we'll continue to get the results we've always gotten.

To eliminate the clutter, we need to speak unambiguously. We need to talk about what we stand for and against. We need to school ourselves in the basics of the unique political philosophy of the United States and of the modern conservative political philosophy. In short, we must add practical political activism to our deep understanding of human nature.

Conservatives are shocked to meet passionate, outspoken, and boisterous liberals who, on cursory examination, know little or nothing about the subjects they feel so passionately about. We smugly condescend, "Why these people don't even know what they're for or against." Then we're shocked when the other side's policy position wins out over ours.

There are a few statists who command the facts. Very few. Most are people who have simply fallen into line behind a fad that makes them feel good. The statist leaders blanket the airwaves with emotional nonsense that appeals to kindhearted people. Look at some of the rhetoric the left uses in its push for socialized medicine:

We want everyone to have access to affordable healthcare

We want you to keep your insurance if you like it

We want to reduce the cost of healthcare

We want to free you from the worry that you'll lose your healthcare if you lose your job

We want to prevent insurance companies from denying you coverage just because you've had a past illness

This language is effective because it appeals to our emotions. No one wants to watch someone die in pain for want of $2,000 worth of procedures and medicine. The left says that if you oppose socialized medicine, though, you're effectively tying a plastic bag over the heads of the poor. It's balderdash, but it strikes an emotional cord with the large number of people who don't live and breathe politics.

The mistake Conservatives make is to counter the liberal arguments with logical ones. Faced with the barrage of messages above, Conservatives would respond:

- I never said I wanted to deny people treatment

- We don't want people to worry about losing insurance . . .
- We don't want insurance prices to skyrocket . . .
- The free market allows more innovation . . .
- There is no healthcare crisis in America
- The Constitution . . .

All of these arguments lose people who are *not* politically attuned. The reason: these phrases are either a) defensive or b) logical. Studies have shown that logical, rational advertising does not work. Emotional advertising, when devoid of any rational arguments, is twice as effective as rational advertising, according to a study by Roger Dooley of Neuromarketing.com:

> Campaigns with purely emotional content performed about twice as well (31% vs. 16%) [as those] with only rational content, and those that were purely emotional did a little better (31% vs 26%) those that mixed emotional and rational content. (2009)

Yet Conservatives continue to clutter their arguments and advertising with appeals to reason. We justify our obstinacy by saying "we shouldn't have to let go of our traditional words like liberty, Constitution, etc. People should respond to these words."

Perhaps. But should isn't real. For 50 years, educators, entertainers, reporters, and statist politicians have told the country that only rightwing lunatics care about the Constitution. As a result, many people are turned off simply by hearing words like "liberty," "Constitutional," "enumerated powers," and "tenth amendment." These people—the 70 percent who do not feel tightly bound to any party or ideology—want to avoid discord and argument. When a Conservative says, "Liberty," they hear, "a fight is starting" and mentally run away; they stop paying attention.

So let it go. If using the word "Liberty" means that fewer people will support our ends **don't use the word "liberty,"** for God's sake! If "healthcare system" turns off the undecided, don't say it. By insisting on using words that don't work with people, you are letting your personal battle interfere with our war against tyranny. That makes YOU a problem, not a solution. You might feel good for an hour having pounded your chest like proud and fearless Silverback gorilla, but you have lost votes for the very thing you support.

Instead, find out what the working words are. Conservative pollster, Dr. Frank Luntz does phenomenal work finding out the words and phrases that inspire the 70 percent in the so-called middle. He publishes his findings regularly.

During the great socialized medicine debate of the summer of 2009, he released a paper titled "The Language of Healthcare 2009."

Until I read that paper, I had been writing about the issue almost daily using words that I like: free markets, capitalism, liberty, Constitution, Tenth Amendment, enumerated powers, Article I, etc. I was too damn proud to use words that people in the middle might respond to. "Screw that political correctness crap," I said.

Then I thought about it more deeply and away from the raging fights of the day. I realized that my attitude could sink free markets and capitalism. If we didn't find a way to appeal to the majority who just want cheaper healthcare and less fighting, the other side surely would. The choice was between Liberty and Tyranny; my pride could not get in the way.

So I wrote a blog post on the subject using Frank Luntz's language but my arguments. There results were astounding. In the first 24 hours, that post was forwarded or bookmarked more then 2,000 times. That might not be much for Gateway Pundit or one of the powerhouse blogs, but that was greater than 15 times more "shares" than any post I'd written to that point. The right words, with an emotional appeal based on solid facts and truths, will move the middle toward the right.

Because Americans are inclined toward conservatism, we only have to tie the left in quality of arguments. We don't have to trump them. Our message must appeal to emotions, supported by rational facts. We must be able to pull up those facts and argue rationally when the time is right, but our message must be emotional because humans are not rational in the normal understanding of that word. If we were, there would be no economic bubbles.

Offer Solutions

Every conservative should have a tongue-ready list of at least 5 reforms he or she would implement immediately if given the authority. Reporters generally will not investigate deeper once you rattle off five reforms, but it's smart to have at least 3 pillars of facts to support each reform. For example, I would cut the corporate income tax rate to 12.5 percent from 35 percent. First, at 12.5 percent our tax rate would not be the lowest in the industrialized world, but it would be near the bottom, equaling Ireland's. Second, the reason corporations spend millions of dollars setting up off-shore bank accounts is to avoid an onerous tax rate in the United States. Cutting the rate, alone, would destroy the return on investment in managing off-shore accounts, increasing the amount of money on which U.S. corporations pay tax. Third, a tax rate of 12.5 percent would increase internal investment, increase revenue and profits, and ultimate increase total federal revenue from corporate taxes, just as large cuts in the marginal individual rates have resulted in increased, not decreased, tax revenue *every time it's been done.*

Let the leftists live in the world of economic theory; we'll take the hard cold fact that rate cuts cause revenue increases. As Ronald Reagan once said, if a economist sees something happening in the real world, he'll immediately apply for a grant to study whether or not it will work in theory.

While you should focus on one or two policy areas, five reforms is something of a magic number. For two policy areas, divide your reforms 3 to 2.

Test Everything Against The Ultimate Question

Catholic theologian Michael Novak gave us the ultimate question a quarter century ago: "Will it *liberate*?"

Novak applied the question to liberation theology in a brilliant 1987 book. The resounding answer: "No."

Liberation is most often achieved by doing less, which is why secular Zen so beautifully exposes this kernel of conservatism. But the question soon arises, "How do we know *it* liberates?"

Human beings are endowed by their Creator with certain unalienable rights, one of which is liberty. Coming from God, it must be good. So what is liberty? Is it the right to do anything I choose? No. That's license, which we covered earlier. Liberty is the right to do anything that's good. You have the ability to sin. You have the ability to do evil--everyone does. But the ability, even the license, to do evil does not make doing evil good.

In order to answer "yes" to the question "will it liberate" the thing must allow, encourage, or enable men to do the good of their own choosing. Now, we could argue for years about what is good, but that would be silly. We already know. There are very few hard questions. Questions seem hard only when we ask them too late.

Have Close Liberal Friends

Both liberals and conservatives have, of late, taken on the despicable habit of vilifying the other. My own blog is no exception. Yet I count among my friends people whose political, religious, and social views vary from mine by nearly 180 degrees. I would trade these friends for nothing, though I wish they would see more things my way.

Maintaining friendships--not just civil acquaintances-- with liberals keeps the mind fresh and nimble, deters the kind of malevolent rhetoric that fills the Internet, and gives you a better understanding of the solutions that will resonate with those who call themselves "liberal" or "progressive."

A cynical sentiment is to have liberal friends because we should keep our enemies close. That way of thinking guarantees little more than short, false friendships. There is a far better reason for conservatives to make and maintain friendships with people we don't agree with.

Right or wrong, the liberal media have successfully painted conservatism as an ideology bursting with anger, frustration, and hatred. When Bill Clinton vetoed a federal budget, Republicans got the blame. When Bill Clinton was caught having an affair with a White House intern, Republicans got the blame. When the stock market sinks, free markets get the blame. When people get killed in war, the military takes the blame.

The liberals I know (and until the tea party movement started, I knew more liberals than conservatives) think I'm some sort of an exception, although I'm not.

I remember sitting one night at a pancake house in St. Louis at 3:00 in the morning with two friends of mine--one liberal and one conservative. The two women were old friends who'd drawn me into their circle.

As we talked over coffee, the liberal woman said, "Why are you a conservative? You're so nice. You smile and laugh all the time."

She was completely sincere. Conservatives, according to her understanding, scowl and lecture, judge and condemn. We beat our kids and kill Bambi's mother from a secluded tree stand, then litter the highway with the animal's entrails before stripping naked at a drunken bonfire and eating the beast's raw flesh from our Bowie knives. (For the record, that happened only once, it was at I time when I was politically ambivalent, and I was coming down with the flu.)

During the week, of course, we make 10 times the national average by exploiting African-Americans and laying off a single mother whose absentee husband fled to Florida with his secretary and a coke dealer after casting his first Republican vote in 1994. We operate hazardous waste dumps near farms and pre-schools to ensure plenty of cancer victims who will later, in desperation, buy our snake-oil supplements falsely promised to cure their particular ailments. We use the proceeds from this swindle to fund our retirements in Jamaica before our 45th birthdays.

As long as we isolate ourselves in Conservative-Only clubs and circles, the only exposure to conservatives that liberals and the politically careless will have are the false stereotypes dreamt up by Hollywood screenwriters bent on paying back the captain of the football team for giving wedgies during study hall in 1989.

Get out and party with the people who weren't fortunate to gain your understanding of the way the world works.

For a time, I attended a Thursday evening happy hour at The a local pub called "The Fox and Hounds" with former co-workers. These kids were hard left, anti-business techies who believed that all music, code, and clothing should be produced and distributed gratis. People should take what they need from the common stockpile and contribute their own unique talent for the betterment of the world. They didn't consider themselves communists; they bristled at the accusation.

I could have refused to lift a glass of 12-year-old single malt Scotch with these kids, 10 years my juniors. But that would have meant denying me the pleasure of their engaging and delightful company. John and Dave (we'll call them) and their girlfriends could make me laugh and think. They kept me sharp at a time when 80-hour weeks of software development management dulled my mind and isolated me from the world beyond my monitor. So I honored the Thursday Scotch and Conversation Club as we called it.

One Thursday, John explained in careful, reasoned paragraphs why Napster was not an illegal music piracy scheme but a portrait of a better future.

"What right," he said, "does a record executive have to deny people the pleasure of music?"

I thought about respondiing directly. Instead, I made a flanking argument.

"You write code for a living, right?" I asked.

"Yeah."

"And until a few months ago, we paid you a pretty decent salary for your code, didn't we?"

"Sure, I guess."

"Why didn't you write the code for free?"

"I'm not stupid. If you're willing to pay for my code, then why wouldn't I take your money?"

"Exactly. And if we weren't willing to pay, would you still have written code?"

"I don't know."

"Well, we had to lay you and a hundred other people off. I promise you that I will get you a badge and a computer and you can come back to work tomorrow as long as we don't have to pay you."

"I gotta eat."

"Don't song writers and musicians have to eat? Shouldn't they be able to tell you that you must pay to hear their music?"

John smiled. While he could have sparred a few more rounds, he knew that his case was lost. He defeated himself by admitting that he wrote code because his employer paid him; he denied us his talent when the offer was rescinded.

Had I decided, on some principle, not to hang around with liberals or communists, this conversation would never have taken place.

John, I'm sure, is still a liberal and a Democrat. I'm 99 percent sure he voted for Barack Obama and John Kerry. I'm sure he continues to work for his local Democrat club and party. But I also know he believes a man is owed a day's wage for a day's work, that a worker is entitled to the fruits of labor. He might be okay with government confiscating a portion of that wage for redistribution to others, but I'll bet he's a little more suspicious of "spread the wealth" programs than he was before that particular Thursday.

Liberal friends can also teach us. We learn why they think as they do. We learn, for instance, that most liberals base their world view on an emotional desire to be free from negative feelings. It's a sincere reaction, but it's hardly a noble one. Their goal is not so much to alleviate the suffering of the unfortunate, but to feel no guilt. In this desire to avoid guilt, they invent wrongs that have afflicted them. "I'm a victim, too," they say. It's nonsense, but they say it so often that they end up believing it. Pretty soon you have a Jeanine Garofalo on your hands. You'll need something stronger than Dial soap to get that stain out.

Engaging these feelings, we can effectively visualize a world where suffering, though present, is relieved by the altruistic kindness and compassion of individuals. Instead of hiring a faceless bureaucrat to make bad things simply go away (or go somewhere else), we can take direct action to help those who need our help.

This direct action can extend beyond the suffering of specific individuals. If a large number of people refuse to buy the products of companies that practice wicked treatment of employees or that dump toxins into the local pond, the companies will have to clean up their acts or cease to exist. Either way the problem stops.

Liberals in modern times, instead, take action to get *the government* to do something about it. They raise awareness in hopes more and more people will *demand government action*. They get the courts to do their bidding. How often have heard (or said), "Someone should do something about this!" Or, "There should be a law . . . ." In a better-ordered society, you'd hear (or say), "Dammit, *I'm* going to do something about this." For example, if pollution and exploitation bother you, how long are you willing to wait for government to stop them? Polluters and exploiters are experts at resisting legislation and lawsuits. A campaign contribution here or a loophole there, and the legislative hurdle goes away. But the same companies cannot long ignore their customers. Eventually, two bad quarters get the board's attention, the management team gets pink slips (and golden parachutes), and a new CEO changes the company's practices. Government just isn't that effective.

Perhaps the most compelling reason for making and keeping liberal friends is this: they must be enjoyable for us to befriend them.

Normal, well-adjusted people don't hang around with people they don't personally like. That's not to say we don't have friends who get on our nerves or who have annoying habits. It certainly doesn't mean we agree with all our friends' politics. But there is something about our friends that makes us seek out their company.

Why should we deny ourselves the frequent pleasure of enjoyable people? Life is too damn short to spend it in isolation because we can't find anybody who agrees with our distinct and carefully analyzed interpretation of the Magna Carta's significance to wage-pull inflation in the early 1970s.

Savor Freedom

Five is a lot of kids these days.

"You have five kids? Oh, my God!" people say, their eyes bugged out, mouths wide open.

Even when the oldest were babies, developmental psychologists were advising parent not to tell children "no." Their theory was that "no" would teach the child limitations and destroy his curiosity. Instead, offer an alternative. (Well, that doesn't work.)

But the funny thing is, it's the no "no" advice that is totally out of synch with society.

My dad came home from two wars: World War II and Korea. On quiet evenings, I sometimes try to think to of the prohibitions Jack Hennessy faced in 1953. He changed the oil in his car, smoked in the grocery store and Sears, drove a car without a seatbelt, built a house to own liking, spanked his kids when they had it coming, let his 16-year-old kids swim without a lifeguard, rode a bike without a helmet, flew the American flag, and washed his car in the driveway.

These are just a few of the things his grandchildren can't do. And the list of "NO"s gets longer every day, doesn't it. For instance, his son, according McCain-Feingold, cannot blog 60 days before an election. Petty little pleasures aren't they, which society denies us? And it denies more every day.

It saddens me when I read young people's blogs that seem to encourage the government to deny more freedoms. They seem willing, even eager, to trade their little bits of freedom for some guarantee of health, wealth, and happiness. How sad. And how naive. Of course, their little pieces of freedom are so puny by 1953 standards, it's no wonder they're willing to cast them aside. Sam Adams and George Washington knew some serious freedom; they were eager to die to preserve it for their kids.

And absolute prohibitions are only the start of our freedoms denied. You can't do a lot of things without money, so another way society limits our freedom—places more "NO"s on us—is taxation. When Dad came home from Korea, combined taxes were 25 percent of GNP. Today, the percentage of the economy that goes to taxes is almost 40 percent. That's a lot of freedom transferred from the people to the politicians.

There are dangers in driving without a seat belt, shooting off fireworks, and swimming in a river. There is life in these things, too. They are pursuits of happiness to many. There is excitement and rush and flush and pleasure. There is childhood and feeling grown up. There is joy and memory and anticipation and running through the woods at night laughing with your friends. There is freedom. And maybe real freedoms would make the escapism of recreational drugs and careless sex less attractive. Maybe young people today would act more like kids in the 50s if they were allowed to act like kids in the 50s.

Freedom. Cherish it, cultivate it, pass it on in greater abundance than you found it.

Ultimately, this is all about freedom—freedom from the arbitrary rule of other men. Freedom from the whims of an elected official or appointed judge. As Mark Steyn told Hillsdale College recently, despotism is always whimsical.

There's no point in achieving liberty if we're too timid or too angry or too vengeful to pursue happiness.

We must also be willing to accept happiness when it arrives.

Be Cheerful

This is perhaps the most important trait of all. People loved Ronald Reagan because he was cheerful. He was also humble. He was also focused. Why would anyone adopt a political ideology when that ideology's most visible promoters come off as bitter, hostile, mean, and angry?

When California voters approved a ballot proposition banning gay marriage in the state, gay activists went berserk. They attacked Christian women on the streets, threatened Mormons, and rioted. My guess is that their behavior inspired no one of sound mind to support their cause.

By contrast, the day after the 2008 election, conservative talk show host Rush Limbaugh sounded ecstatic. He was happy and delighted to have a great job with ridiculously high income. He speaks his mind every day while millions of people listen, nod their heads, and call in to echo or extend his remarks. Rush has an abiding faith in the American experience and people: no matter how badly the Obama administration damages liberty, we will rise again. Obama can shroud the shining city on the hill, but the candles inside will eventually burn away the cloth.

Watch Your Virtues

Too much of a good thing, as my mother would say, turns bad.

When Chesterton wrote "Orthodoxy" in 1908, he looked at his modern times and pitied their unimaginative banality. He would surely weep aloud were he to observe our times.

"The modern world," he wrote a century ago, "is full of the old Christian virtues gone mad. The virtues have gone mad because they have been isolated from each other and are wandering alone."

With two easy sentences, Chesterton sums up the whole leftist nutroots thing. Among these nutroots, you will find every Christian virtue evolved freakishly unrecognizable through intellectual incest. The virtues, any combination, depend upon each other. Love becomes onerous unless balanced with Hope and Faith. Courage results in movies like "Jack Ass" unless combined with Justice, Prudence, and Temperance. Justice without Temperance and Prudence is al Qaeda. And any virtue turns evil without Humility.

In Cindy Sheehan, we see complete loss of humility. She believed her own press, and now challenges the woman without whom her own anonymity would be complete.

In PETA, we see the virtue of kindness run amok, turned evil by its isolation from humility and liberality.

The whole green thing and global warming mania have turned the virtue of humility into an affront against reason.

The Catholic Encyclopedia explains that virtues must be connected to each other:

Another property of virtues is their connection with one another. This mutual connection exists between the moral virtues in their perfect state. "The virtues", says St. Gregory, "if separated, cannot be perfect in the nature of virtue; for that is no true prudence which is not just and temperate and brave".

Individual virtues are isolated on the right, as well, and quite frequently right here in my writings and actions. How often am I challenged, not by enemies on the left but allies on the right, for allowing courage or justice to run unfettered by humility and temperance?

"A man was meant to be doubtful about himself, but undoubting about the truth," said Chesterton; "this has been exactly reversed."

These virtues *cum* vices, through their isolation from one another, led modern man beyond the end of reason. If we may doubt the truth, we must doubt all else. If a thing can be doubted, it must be ignored. If God Himself is doubtable, my thoughts must be mistaken. This absurd line of reasoning ends, Chesterton tells us, with the negative reverse of Descartes' famous postulation: "I am not; therefore, I cannot think."

I will try to remember to practice the seven virtues—faith, hope, charity, prudence, justice, temperance, and fortitude—more connectedly. Perhaps the best we can all do, we who hope to preserve that great Western Judeo-Christian ideal, is to insist the same from the leaders of the modern movements.

But the real danger posed by isolated virtue becoming rampant vice stems from the left, not the right. While we may have flaws, ours are of degree— theirs are of kind.

We must hold up statists to their own standards. They must prove that their "cure" is preferable to the ailment. They must prove that their legislation is legal in the eyes of the Constitution and its ratifiers. They must convince the world that their solutions will liberate.

What You Can Do

If you read a blog post on on www.stlouisteaparty.com that seems to be rooting for America to fail or suffer in order that Obama take the blame, please e-mail me (bill-at–hennessysview–dot–com) and comment. I'm a hot-head, and I might not catch myself.

The United States and every country on earth stand in a perilous position right now. The world economy remains on the brink of depression. Bad business practices driven by even worse government policies and regulations have destroyed trillions of dollars in wealth and left us on a narrow, swampy peninsula between deflation and hyperinflation.

We have, for good or ill, elected a young and inexperienced president. That man's past rhetoric was clearly Marxist. But his post-election appointments and words seemed closer to those of George Bush than to Gus Hall's. We can work to win back Congress and the White House without destroying the country in the process. Here are a few recommendations:

- Acknowledge the administration's rightward tacks as publicly as you attack its leftist moves

- Look for people or businesses in your area who need help and help them if you can
- State the positive results of conservative governance more often than you assail the consequences of statist error
- Wave to drivers of cars with Obama stickers, even as you pass them. That way they're sure to see your Tea Party sticker
- Write letters to the editor, blog comments, and blog posts complimenting Obama's good judgment when he shows it, but always identify yourself as a conservative who will work for his defeat in 2012
- Join the Tea Party Movement

Ronald Reagan said about missile reduction agreements with the Soviet Union: "Trust . . . but verified." While keeping a civil tongue, we must remember that Obama is at heart a statist, if not a a devoted Marxist. He would have supported Castro, though he would not have lived in the hills with Che. He would have praised Mao, though he would have joined the Long March only at the very end.

Obama is the Lincoln Steffens, the I. F. Stone, of politics. His heroes have always been Commies, and they still are, it seems. So, while civility is due, we should give him no quarter. He is our ideological enemy. He is armed and extremely dangerous. Like a snake, Barack H. Obama is a poisonous reptile who remains most dangerous while unseen. The cold, remorseless light of day does not defang him, but it does take away his ability to surprise.

While we work to defend our country and our free enterprise world by protecting our own self-interest, we strive to maximize our net worth without denying others the same opportunity. Understanding that wealth is not a fixed sum from which we each draw a portion, we feel no guilt about earning more tomorrow than we took home today, so long as we've earned our wage fairly and honestly. We are not Democrats who steal, legally or not, from whomever they please, and then tell the victims to think of the children. We are conservatives who earn our recompense and, we hope, spend it wisely.

All of us are saying goodbye to co-workers let go because of the economy. The way out of this mess is lower taxes, less government, and graceful ends for companies that can't make it. Each of these right actions carries with it painful consequences for some of us. We can and must make these changes to our national direction. But we can and should make them without being asses.

We all know how painful and maddening it was to hear statists cheer American casualties in Iraq and fantasize about the assassination of a Republican president. While we might not go so far, why take the chance? Let's sell our superior system of economics and limited government. The deficiencies of their alternative will become glaringly obvious soon enough.

How to Focus: The 5-2-1 Plan

At the Tax Day Tea Party on April 15, 2009, I ended my remarks by asking everyone to take a 5-2-1 challenge. Those tasks were:

- Have things you would change were you in charge, and know them like the back of your hand
- Tell two people that you attended the Tea Party and why
- Write one letter to the editor, to a member of congress, or to a magazine telling them you will do everything in your power to stop the unfettered growth of the government and debt

That formula struck a chord with many, but the last two points are not sustainable. Moreover, they don't help us simplify and focus, which is the key element of this work.

What will help, though, is narrowing our daily behaviors to a specific few that will have the greatest impact. At the same time, we can free up some of our time to do more important things, like raising our families, advancing our careers, or protesting the SEIU.

Have Five New Sources

Choose from these or find your own. But try to limit your daily "must reads" to five. The links within those 5, if they are well written, will take you to hundred very quickly. But have 5 to start your information session.

Remember not to over do it. Spending 8 hours a day on the internet will make you paranoid and afraid. That's a combination that plays into the statists' hands, because the paranoia will make you say silly things and the fear will drive into your home. We need you on the streets and in the shops saying brilliant things (like, "You *must* read 'Zen Conservatism.'")

Here are a few of my favorite launching points. If you use Google Chrome browser (my favorite) or the Google add-in for IE or FireFox, you'll have a handy little landing page that displays thumbnails of the 8 web sites you visit most often. It's a great tool to focus your attention.

MinuteManBlog.org

TownHall.com

GatewayPundit.firstthings.com

HotAir.com

BigGovernment.com,   BigHollywood.com, Breitbart.com

DanaRadio.com

Any of the sites and blogs in the
StLouisTeaParty.com blog roll

FoxNews.com

DrudgeReport.com

MichelleMalkin.com

Ace.mu.nu

TcotReport.com

You get the idea.

Have 2 causes you support with your time and money, if you're so inclined

You don't have to. But if you do, pick one or two, not 30 (unless you're George Soros). Why?

Concentrate your power. Donating $20 a month to Heritage Foundation gives them $240 a year to educate and train the next generation of politicians. Dividing that $240 among 10 organizations focused each on different things dilutes your investment to tiny batches of $24 scattered all over the political landscape.

What are the 2 issues or needs you feel the most passion about?

Ask yourself this during election years: is there a candidate deserves every penny you can spare? If you're sending $5 a month to 10 different organizations, you probably can't afford to send $100 to the guy running against a prominent liberal when the challenger needs it most. You'll be tapped out.

Zen is about focus. Focus your contributions on the two things you're most passionate about. Someone else will fund the other things that fall farther down on your list. And if they don't, let the market work. Causes and issues that do not attract funding probably aren't that important.

Here is just a short list of some of my favorite causes and groups:

Heritage Foundation (www.heritagefoundation.org)

Cato Institute (www.cato.org)

Political Parties (www.rnc.org; www.dnc.org)

National Right to Life (www.nrlc.org)

Birthright (www.birthright.org)

National Review (www.nationalreview.com)

Your local Tea Party (Web search "tea party" + [your city or state])

A political candidate who endorses the Tea Party or the 9-12 Project.

Spend at least 1 hour every week working on a grassroots organization

In the St. Louis area, we have more than a dozen outstanding organizations that promote conservatism, Judeo-Christian values, small government, low taxes, Constitutional constraint, or combinations thereof. These groups are the lifeblood of the St. Louis Tea Party movement. They run the checklists, call the meetings, hock the spirit wear, and activate the phone tree for events big and small.

In a metropolis like St. Louis, you need the connectedness that groups like these provide. They remind me of church congregations the way the look out for each other, help wherever they can, ask always, "what else can I do," and never, "it's somebody else's turn."

I'll bet you can find these groups in your area, too. They'll have little tables set up at the nearest Tea Party or 9-12 Project event. But if you can't find them, start your own. Get a small group of like-minded folks together at your house or a neighborhood tavern. Give yourselves a name. Create a social networking site on www.ning.com, and tell your few members that job one is to recruit 2 new members each. Within a month or two of bi-weekly meetings, you'll need a room at a public library or city hall to hold everyone.

Then, get out and take action. Make appointments, one by one, with members of your federal Congressional delegation. Sit down with your Representative's or Senator's staff and tell them how you feel. Even if your Congressman is Bernie Sanders, tell them how you feel. Your representatives deserve to hear from you, and you deserve to be heard.

Make sure the Tea Party or 9-12 organizers in your area know about your group. Offer to work your phone tree when there's an event coming up. Help to take up initiatives when the larger organization can't move fast enough.

If your area does not have a consolidated Conservative Calendar, create one. Google Calendar (calendar.google.com) is a great tool. Make one or two leaders of each center-right organization an administrator. Then embed that calendar into all of the organizations' web sites. Now, everyone can go to a single calendar to find out what's going on. This will help increase attendance and avoid one organization stepping on another's toes.

Also, pick candidates who deserve all of your support. While we'd all like to vote for perfect candidates, we've never had that option. Instead, follow

William F. Buckley's advice by supporting the rightward-most viable candidate. Please don't skip any words in that phrase: rightward-most *viable* candidate. In 2008, Fred Thompson was the rightward-most, viable candidate until about the South Carolina primary. He remained "rightward-most" but lost the "viable" thing. Then it was John McCain. Ron Paul was never viable.

In 1992, the rightward-most, viable candidate was George H. W. Bush, not Ross Perot. While the Paul voters didn't detract from McCain's chances last year, Perot voters gave us Bill Clinton. And remember this: most of the time, if a 3rd party candidate's philosophy is closely aligned to yours, voting for him can only increase the chances of electing the candidate most ideologically different from you. In short, KNOCK OFF THE THIRD PARTY CRAP! Don't let ideological purity cause you to help a statist get elected. Of the two major parties, only one openly advances Marxist.

Some people are whirlwinds who seem to thrive on having lots to do. Political marketing master, Gina Loudon, likes to say, "if you want to get something done, give it to the busiest person you know." But not everyone is a whirlwind. Moreover, many whirlwinds are already at the breaking point even before thinking adding political activism to their workload.

For the rest of us, we need to be careful that we don't overreach. Overreach causes two problems.

1. A lot gets done, but the work is of poor quality.
2. The person burns out quickly.

Either way, the job's left undone. Meaningful action takes time. Victories are small and the valleys that separate one peak from another are wide and dangerous. Doing things half-way or quitting early stops momentum.

When the Tea Party movement started on February 22, we had one goal: get 50 people to show up at the Arch the following Friday. As I've already mentioned, fifteen hundred showed up. That was a victory, but a tiny one. We had not changed a single vote or seat in Congress. The President was the most radical leftist ever elected to the White House. Our victory consisted of learning that at least 1,499 other people were as worried as we were.

The next victory was April 15 when 10,000 people attended the St. Louis rally and over 1.2 million attended Tea Parties nationally. A week later, Barack Obama slipped and addressed the tea parties directly. Even this victory, though, was minor. We received a lot of attention. We bothered the President. A core group of activists began emerging. We proved we could attract large crowds on almost zero budgets. But Stimulus passed and Cap & Trade and Healthcare were coming fast.

Luckily, most of the planners and organizers did a great job of keeping each other focused. When one of us (usually me) would stray into issues beyond the Tea Party's focus, the others would nudge us back to fiscal responsibility through strict adherence to the enumerated powers of the Constitution.

Had we strayed into other important issues like the Second Amendment or immigration, the success we had in fighting socialized medicine in July and August never would have happened. With diffused focus, we would have addressed many issues poorly and without effect. With focus, we were able significantly limit the ability of statists to advance socialized medicine before the 2010 election. [As of this writing, the Administration appears to have abandoned the so called "public option."]

While too many causes and issues result in ineffectiveness or burnout, two few can become monotonous. Single focus may make people feel ineffectual. The 5-2-1 method balances these two extremes. Moreover, five web sites, two groups, and one grassroots cause will allow you to continue the other part of your life. There may be some adjustments required, but you should be able to handle a career and a mission.

This last point is critical for conservatives. Liberals pay people to protest, to write letters, to harass conservatives, to draw conservatives into fights, to sue conservatives. In short, liberalism is professional activism. They see themselves first as agents of socialism, or statism, and all other aspects of their lives as necessary distractions. Their goal is to force you and me to pay them to steal more of our money.

Conservatives have a more ordered understanding of life's purpose. We organize or attend Tea Parties so we can barbeque later. We work to make money to enjoy our free time and to educate our kids. We go to church (I hope) to become closer to God. We engage in political activism to retain as much of the freedom God gave as we choose to keep.

This means we need 1.2 conservatives to effect the same amount of change as a single liberal. Pulling in your friends and family is all the more critical to our cause because we need more of us than there are of them. In addition to the 5-2-1, regular recruiting is our constant duty.

My 1993 book intended to activate conservatives. It was a manifesto of rightwing political action. It sold nearly 20,000 copies over three and a half years. Others with far more talent better brains wrote similar tomes at the same time. What happened?

Well, we might take some satisfaction in the 1994 Congressional election. In that historical year, Newt Gingrich led a band of conservatives to victory in the House and Senate. The brilliant Contract with America identified 10 reforms that the GOP slate promised to bring to a floor vote within 100 days of the start of Congress. Five of the 10 items became law. All 10 made it to an up or down vote. Among the new laws was welfare reform, the most sweeping recovery of Constitutional power since the Alien and Sedition acts were repealed.

Unfortunately, no perpetual movement began as a result of the 1994 Republican sweep. The first sign of trouble in the GOP came in 1996, when the party nominated the centrist had-been, Bob Dole as its standard-bearer.

Now, Bob Dole is a good man, a patriot, and an able legislator. He lost the use of hand in Italy during World War II, and he dedicated his life to making America a better country.

He was also the epitome of the beltway. Bob Dole cut deals like a lumberjack cuts trees. Dole has no problem expanding the scope of government without the consent of the states or the people when it suits him. He was a me-too conservative who backed Ronald Reagan into a corner in 1982, forcing Reagan to sign a tax increase. (Jack Kemp, Dole's 1996 running mate, in 1986 overrode Dole's tax increase before it did any real harm to the economy.)

After the 1996 election, things actually got worse. With the economy about to skyrocket thanks to the tech bubble (artificial) and welfare reform (authentic), Republicans focused on the Monica Lewinsky scandal. A distraction. A big one. A damaging one. When Republicans weren't making too much of the President's infidelity, they became obsessed with money. Conspicuous consumption of the late 1990s made the Reagan Era look like Mother Teresa's convent. That was us, folks. Many of us, anyway, and my hand is as high in the air as I can get it. Blame me.

If we skip over the year 2000 and the first 4 years of GWB, we come to the hideous night in 2006. Know how screwed up Bush's second term was? Harry Reid and Nancy Pelosi looked like winners to the American public. That's pretty screwed up. In fact, here's what I wrote at the time:

> In November 1994, I was still writing for TownHall.com. At about 11:00 p.m. CST, I retired to my office on the second floor, scotch and cigars in hand, and typed out what I consider my best column ever: Runnymede Revisited. [That column was lost when a

computer malfunction wiped out Town Hall's archives a few years ago.]

The gist of the piece was that Newt Gingrich and the Republicans, with the help of the American people, had re-enacted the forced signing of the Magna Carta. Democracy was again legal. All was not lost.

Tonight, I cannot help but think King John signed the document with disappearing ink. Twelve years hence, we have very little to show for the Republican avalanche of 1994. President Bush has woefully mismanaged Iraq, resulting in unnecessary American and Iraqi deaths. The federal government has grown faster than Johnson might have dreamed of growing it. Our borders are more porous than in 1980. Congress is gone.

President Bush has two years to fix some of the damage he's done in the previous two. His first administration was admirable, if not conservative, but his second has been an unmitigated disaster. Save for his two Supreme Court appointments, Bush has nothing to show for his second term but flag-draped coffins and enemies in Congress.

I still support the war. I hope Bush will finally decide to win the damn thing instead of piddling around like a business executive re-ordering PowerPoint slides before the board meeting. We need 250,000 troops on the ground with orders to kill anything that looks suspicious. Don't worry—all will be forgiven when final victory comes home with the troops.

He needs to acknowledge in no uncertain terms, "I f***ed up. I said that I had a lot of political capital that I intended to spend. I didn't spend it, so much as I pissed it away. I get it, people. And swear I will use these remaining two years to fix every problem I made."

And if he has a strategic bone in his body, he'll add, "So ask your Representative and Senators to help me win the war for civilization, to put government beneath the people, and to find that son of a bitch bin Laden and hang his miserable ass from the roof of the White House."

Finally, let's not be too hard on ourselves. Whether we are conservatives or Republicans or Democrats or libertarians or objectivists or just plain Americans, we don't want to spend every free moment plotting some tactic to mess with the left. We don't want government on our minds 24 hours a day.

The reason Washington, Adams, Madison, Hamilton, and all the founders devised a limited government was to free people from thinking about government. Like you and me, Washington wanted to mount his steed and trot back to Mount Vernon, pour himself a gin and tonic, and kick back with Martha and the grandkids. He didn't want to spend his remaining years tweaking the Fed funds rate or sneaking earmarks for Virginia into a continuing resolution.

Yes, we on the right have repeatedly dropped the ball, kicked it, let the other side run up the score, and watched helplessly as the officials missed every statist foul while giving them 5 downs and us four. Yes, it's late in the third quarter, we're down by 8, and the statists have the ball on our side of the 50 yard line. And, yes, it's entirely our fault for politically slacking, nominating boring white guys, and making our best candidates (like Jack Kemp and Sarah Palin) the undercards of losing tickets. Yes, we've screwed up.

But isn't that the essence of "pursuit of Happiness?" Haven't we precisely lived out that beautiful ideal that Jefferson penned for us in 1776? "The pursuit of Happiness" is why we are conservatives, libertarians, and Republicans. It's why we strive to make America better. It's why we demand low taxes and light regulation. We want to pursue happiness on our terms. Babysitting Congress is not on our bucket list.

The ebb and flow of history is as old as walking upright and hunting Wooly Mammoths. Leftists grow the government, screw up Europe, jack taxes through the roof, crash the economy, emasculate the military, and piss off two-thirds of the world. To liberals, meddling in other people's business — and charging them for it — is almost instinctive. And because this pathology is *activist* in nature, it only takes a few statists to throw the whole balance of power thing completely out of whack.

But history shows that there is a countervailing pattern, and this counter-flow is our duty. In the counter-flow, normal, sane people come riding in at the last possible moment—when Hitler's bombing London, when Iran has 83 hostages, when Clinton's seizing the healthcare industry—and we save the world. We institute a freeze on government growth; we sort out what the hell's going on; we cut taxes to get things moving again; we eliminate 298 wasteful and unnecessary federal programs and agencies; we win a landslide re-election. Then, of course, we tend to pop the champagne, put on silly elephant hats, and get big, cushy jobs on K Street sitting right next to Tom Daschle and his wife.

Right now, of course, there's more at risk than just hospitals, nurses, doctors, medical schools, and your life. This particular president and his minions in Congress seem determined to end the American Experiment on Khrushchev's terms. The very existence of the American Ideal is on the block. The ball is on our 30, and even a field goal would break our backs just now.

So stiffen up, patriots, and hold the line. We're going to sack their quarterback, bury their ball carriers behind the line, and shiver the fillings out of their receivers' teeth. We've forced the left to fumble in the past; we just haven't been in position to recover the ball. Or we've gone three-and-out after recovering.

This time, though, the stakes are through the roof. This is sudden death. When we take back that ball, we must remember that we're still trailing. We have to score, recover an on-side kick, then score again.

So buckle your chin-straps. This time, we play for keeps.

Appendix 1: The Conservative Creed
Reprinted from "The Conservative Manifesto"

We believe that governments exist at the will of and to serve the governed.

We believe that a government's only powers are those surrendered to it by those it governs, and that the governed may, at any time, reclaim their powers or deny the government of them.

We believe that the individual is free to do as he wishes within the rules set forth by the majority of his fellow citizens and their elected representatives.

We believe that individuals have the right to speak their minds on all political matters.

We believe that individuals have the right to life.

We believe that economic freedom is equal to all other freedoms and the beginning of individual liberty; that government shall not impede economic transactions; and that the power of economic decision resides exclusively with the individual.

We believe that individuals have the right to own personal property and to dispose of that property as they wish.

We believe that identifiable groups have no rights superior to those of the individual, that no group is exempt from the laws deemed right by the majority, and that government may not favor one group before another or before the individual.

We believe that rule of the majority is absolute in all political matters.

We believe that government should not prevent individuals from failing.

We believe that government should not prevent individuals from achieving.

We believe that government's first responsibility is the protection of its citizens and their property, and that when the government fails to provide such protection, it is the right of the citizens to protect themselves.

We believe that policy decisions should be based on the principle of whether the policy will liberate or bind the individual.

We reject the principle of equality of outcome, but demand equality of opportunity.

We reject the notion of superior rights for certain individuals.

We reject the right of a government to increase its own power without the consent of the governed.

We reject the notion of a right to be free from offensive political speech.

We reject the principle of perfectibility of man but believe the individual pursuit of perfection paramount to a good society.

We reject the right of a minority faction to thwart the will or overthrow the government of the majority.

We resist surrendering individual power to the state.

A common language being crucial to achieving harmony, we reject the idea of government mandated multilingualism, but acknowledge the right of individuals to remain ignorant of English.

We acknowledge that education must be promoted and pursued; that government should promote Judeo-Christianity and remain neutral toward other religions; that individuals have different talents and will achieve according to those talents and the diligence with which they are applied if the individual is left alone; that individuals will fail from time to time despite attempts of governments to prevent it; that our achievements are possible only because of the works of generations which came before us; that we are morally responsible to preserve our freedoms for our posterity; that individuals are morally compelled to assist the advancement of society; that work is morally required of all those who benefit from the society; and that, from time to time, individuals must lend more of their power to the government in order that it may meet the needs of emergencies.

Finally, we believe that the course of history has bestowed upon us unparalleled opportunity and responsibility for the protection, nurturing, and advancement of Western Civilization.

Appendix 2: A Message from the Constitution

Those of us whose conservative conversions occurred in the late 1970s and early 1980s, I think, are particularly fascinated by the 10th Amendment to the Constitution. We also mourn over its senseless destruction by Congress, courts, and citizens.

> The powers not delegated to the United States by the Constitution, nor prohibited by it to the States, are reserved for the States respectively, or to the people.

How simple. How refreshing. How freedom-loving. For those whose civics classes centered around Native-American rights and women's suffrage lectures, the straightforward concept of this amendment may be too simple to grasp. Try this:

The Constitution speaking to the new members of the 110th Congress, introducing herself:

"I am the Constitution of the United States of America. I was born September 17, 1787 and baptized by the several states in 1789. My husbands have all died, leaving me to fend for myself. I see you have their portraits and statues adorning your walls and this great city. Thank you. I miss them, too.

"I'd like you to meet my 10th son, born in a litter of 10, in 1791. Being the runt of the litter, he is, of course, my favorite. (Please don't tell the others, though; I love them, too. Even the 14th, who is so shamefully misunderstood by everyone.)"

"The Tenth, as we call him, speaks directly to you and to that court a few blocks from here. But do they listen? Do you hear what he tells you?

"When I see the way you ignore him, I think of Scrooge with the Ghost of Christmas Future. Remember the little boy and little girl huddled under the robe of the grim reaper? Remember what Scrooge's guide told him about them?

'This boy is Ignorance. This girl is Want. Beware them both, and all of their degree, but most of all beware this boy, for on his brow I see that written which is Doom, unless the writing be erased.'

"My Tenth, poor little fellow, warns you the same. You ignore the boy at your own peril. You ignore the writing on his brow—a concept so simple, so easy for you to disregard in your sophistication and achievement and fame. But listen, please, while you still can.

"My Tenth is telling you what his Fathers believed, what you claim in you campaign speeches to believe.

He's talking about me, his mother. He's telling you, 'Listen to my mother!'

"He speaks so softly that you'll need to turn off your iPods and stop the side conversations to hear him. But what he says is, perhaps, more profound than anything ever written. He says, 'If my mother, the Constitution, doesn't tell you, Congress, to do something, it's the same as her telling that you must not do it. Unlike God, Mother doesn't have time to list the things you're not permitted to do—and there are so many. After all, you aren't a creature of God, but of Man. Man is free to do all but a short list of things, but you are permitted to do only that stated in the Constitution, and no more. You are constrained—the people are merely guided.'"

The Congress sat in nervous silence. A few throats cleared. Some people, mostly on the left side of the aisle, looked down at the blue carpet and seemed restless, even angry. They seemed wishing to be adjourned. Others, mostly on the right, seemed to want to hear more, as if they recognized a favorite lullaby their mothers used to sing them. A tiny group, too small to count, really, all on the Right, wept quietly. They loved the Tenth and saw its mother's pain and wondered what its Fathers would say about this and previous Congresses. They knew the Fathers' thoughts would not be kind.

.

5583801R0

Made in the USA
Charleston, SC
06 July 2010